Global Perspectives on Wealth and Distribution

Series Editors

Shirley Johnson-Lans
Vassar College
Poughkeepsie, New York
USA

Feridoon Koohi-Kamali
Emory University
Atlanta, Georgia
USA

This is a broad-ranging and interdisciplinary series dedicated to studying the fundamental economic issue of inequality, including wealth inequality, wage and earnings differentials, and inequality in alternative measures of well-being. The series focuses on studies of developed nations as well as volumes focusing on recent research on inequality in the developing world. Gender- and racial-based inequality and the intra-household division of resources are addressed as well as inequality associated with technological change and globalization and the persistent problem of poverty. The economics of human rights addresses the problems of the most vulnerable members of society and considers policies to alleviate human rights violations.

More information about this series at
http://www.springer.com/series/15384

Shirley Johnson-Lans
Editor

Wage Inequality in Africa

palgrave
macmillan

Editor
Shirley Johnson-Lans
Vassar College
Poughkeepsie
New York, USA

Global Perspectives on Wealth and Distribution
ISBN 978-3-319-51564-9 ISBN 978-3-319-51565-6 (eBook)
DOI 10.1007/978-3-319-51565-6

Library of Congress Control Number: 2017933837

Cover illustration: Pattern adapted from an Indian cotton print produced in the 19th century

Printed on acid-free paper

This Palgrave Macmillan imprint is published by Springer Nature
The registered company is Springer International Publishing AG
The registered company address is: Gewerbestrasse 11, 6330 Cham, Switzerland

Contents

Introduction

Shirley Johnson-Lans

Abstract The studies presented in this book all deal with wage inequality in various African nations. Each addresses a different, but related, aspect of wage inequality. All have something to say about race and/or gender aspects of wage inequality. Each chapter included in this volume is an original empirical research study which attempts to measure and explain sources of wage inequality in the country or countries studied. To conduct such studies, it is necessary to have large national representative samples of households and workers. In each case the authors have used, and in some cases constructed, data sets that meet these requirements.

Keywords Wage inequality · Global perspective · Discrimination · Gender gaps in wages and employment · Racial gender gaps · Urbanization

This book is the first volume of several that are planned on the subject of *Wage Inequality in Developing Countries: A Global Perspective*. As the title of this volume indicates, the studies presented in this book all deal with wage inequality in various African nations. Each addresses a different, but

---

S. Johnson-Lans (✉)
Vassar College, Poughkeepsie, New York, USA

S. Johnson-Lans (ed.), *Wage Inequality in Africa*, Global Perspectives on Wealth and Distribution, DOI 10.1007/978-3-319-51565-6_1

related, aspect of wage inequality. All have something to say about race and/or gender aspects of wage inequality. Each chapter included in this volume is an original empirical research study which attempts to measure and explain sources of wage inequality in the country or countries studied. To conduct such studies, it is necessary to have large national representative samples of households and workers. In each case the authors have used, and in some cases constructed, data sets that meet these requirements.

In building wage determination models it is important to control for worker characteristics that affect productivity, including education and experience, and to control for job-related characteristics that also impact wages such as occupation, industry, location, unionization, urban versus rural, full-/or part-time work, the capital/labor ratio, and the extent of foreign investment in the industry. It is also important to take account of other worker characteristics that may affect wages, and indeed, the likelihood of being in the labor force. These include race and gender (and such things as marital status, size of household, and number of dependent children).

When indicators (dummy variables) for race or gender are included as part of the set of explanatory variables in an estimating equation, their coefficients are often used to measure discrimination. However, since there are always other unexplained factors, some of which may have an impact on worker productivity, all we can safely assert is that the part of the wage differential which manifests itself in the coefficient of 'race' or 'gender' (and in the error term in the equation) is some combination of unobserved worker characteristics and/or discrimination. Obviously the better job the researcher does in isolating all relevant factors, the greater credibility to any assertion of discrimination. However, regardless of the diligence and care with which empirical research is conducted, data sets are always limited, in addition to which some worker characteristics are virtually unobservable.

The research papers in this volume are very conservative in their assertions of discrimination and tend to simply identify the extent to which there are wage differentials associated with race or gender that do not appear to be systematically related to other identifiable factors. The authors tend not to take a stand on what part of observed wage differentials are the result of discrimination, much less delve into the motivation for the alleged discrimination.[1]

The effect of globalization on racial wage differentials in South Africa, specifically the effect of opening the economy to trade and foreign capital, is the central focus of the second chapter. It examines the effect of foreign direct investment (FDI) on racial wage inequality in the immediate post-apartheid decade. This was a time when multinational firms and foreign investors were returning to South Africa after many had departed during the last years of legal apartheid when world public opinion toward this overt racism had become so negative. Attracting foreign capital back into the country was also a conscious policy aim of the post-apartheid government. Theoretically, greater infusions of capital from abroad can either widen or compress wage differentials, or have no effect. Studies of other countries do not provide a consensus of opinion on this matter. Moreover, the relationship between foreign investment and *racial* wage inequality has not attracted much research attention, so this study is an important contribution which furthers our understanding of one of the little studied aspects of globalization. Sectors of the South African economy which experienced greater infusions of FDI are found to have a lower racial wage gap.

The third chapter examines the extent to which major cities in three countries in sub-Saharan Africa manifest an urban wage premium. The study compares Nigeria, Tanzania, and Uganda. The process of urbanization, and the growing importance of the very largest, or primate, cities is a major factor in African economic development. Is location in a large city associated with higher worker productivity, and if so, is it because of an agglomeration effect (higher productivity because of location within the city) or is it because of selection bias, for example, workers who migrate to major cities are different in ways that makes them more productive? This is an important research area since Africa is urbanizing rapidly, and it is therefore crucial to understand the role that cities play in the economic development of the continent. It is also important to understand what groups of workers stand to benefit from an urban wage premium and therefore from migrating to cities. Therefore, understanding the wage structure and the effect on labor productivity of urbanization is a very important research area in both development and labor economics. The study presented in Chapter 3 makes use of large panel data sets covering the years 2009–2013. Three different estimation strategies are used to examine the extent of the urban wage premium and its causes. Tests do not reveal any selection bias that might explain the urban wage premium. However, evidence of an agglomeration effect and a resulting urban wage premium are found, and this phenomenon seems to be primarily a characteristic of wages for workers in primate cities. It is also surprising, since African cities tend not to be manufacturing centers, that the urban wage premium is found to accrue only to male workers.

The fourth chapter examines trends in gender gaps in wages and employment over the first post-apartheid decade in South Africa, when the policies of the new multi-racial democratic government were focused on alleviating racial discrimination. The question is asked, was there any positive spillover from public policy with respect to labor market racial discrimination onto gender discrimination? The study estimates gender gaps in wages separately for each of the three main racial groups: white, colored, and black workers. Comparing men and women of the same race removes some of the unobservable differences in worker characteristics, such as differences in quality of education that may not only reflect differences in quality of schooling but also differences in the social capital of the workers' home communities. A set of two-stage regressions are run in order to isolate the gender component of the wage differential. Stage I regressions make use of individual household and worker information. They generate a set of dependent variables for Stage II which are composed of the coefficients for the control variable 'female' in the Stage I estimations. A similar two-stage strategy is used to examine the trends in ratio of female to male employment over the decade. A series of female/male employment ratios are computed from individual-level data. They become the dependent variables in the Stage II regressions. The findings in this research study indicate that white women appear to be the main group that gained ground in employment over the decade, 1995–2004, whereas the main beneficiaries of a compression in the gender wage gap over this period appeared to be colored women, although some (marginally significant) declines in the gender wage gap were also found for both white and black workers. Reasons for this, including independent evidence from other studies about differential returns to secondary education for non-whites and about the large infusion into the labor force of colored women with secondary education, are examined.

Chapter 3 in this volume covers a set of developing sub-Saharan African countries in which urbanization is of major importance to both the macroeconomic development of the countries and the labor markets, and in which gender is still an important determinant of wage differentials. Although ethnicity may matter a great deal in these three countries, race, defined in terms of color, is not a clear source of wage inequality. By contrast, South Africa has a history of a wage structure that reflected a somewhat different impact of imperialism, namely the high degree of legally sanctioned racial (color) discrimination and segregation in both the work place and living communities that was imposed by the economically dominant white European population and which (legally) ended only in 1994. Studies of both racial and gender wage inequality after the end of formal apartheid in South Africa are thus a major concern of this volume and the subject matter of Chapters 2 and 4.

Note

1. Discrimination may be the result of prejudicial tastes (of employers, fellow workers, or consumers) or it may be 'statistical discrimination'. The latter consists of assigning group characteristics to an individual. If others in the same group have proved to be less productive, then, it might be argued, it is rational for employers to avoid hiring (or promoting) workers from that group or to pay them less if they are hired. For many years such justifications sufficed and whole societies found it rational and acceptable to engage in racial or gender stereotyping. Today, many legal systems, including that of the United States, do not excuse statistical discrimination as somehow less objectionable. It is illegal. However, clearly both taste-based and statistical discrimination are still common in all societies, and statistical discrimination is much harder to eradicate.

Shirley Johnson-Lans is Professor of Economics at Vassar College. Her principal areas of teaching and research are Labor Economics, Health Care Economics, Gender Issues in Economics, and Income Inequality. Her publications include many journal articles and book chapters spanning a wide variety of subjects, from child marriage in rural India to an analysis of the Affordable Care Act. She is the author of the widely used textbook, *A Health Economics Primer* (Pearson: Addison-Wesley, 2006) which she is currently revising. She received her Ph.D. in Economics from Columbia University.

Foreign Direct Investment and Racial Wage Inequality: Evidence from South Africa

Shirley Johnson-Lans and Patricia Jones

Abstract This chapter addresses two questions related to the post-apartheid surge of multinational activity in South Africa. Was the influx of foreign investment associated with a widening or reducing of the wage gap between black and white workers? And second, what impact, if any, has greater foreign investment had on the degree of market concentration in the country? Both questions are investigated using a merged data set from South Africa which covers the period 1995–2004 and thus spans the first decade of democratic government. The results indicate that foreign direct investment (FDI) has been associated with a decrease in the racial wage gap during the post-apartheid decade, more particularly in the first five (Mandela) years.

The authors gratefully acknowledge the support of a Ford Foundation Summer Fellowshop and thank Ford summer fellows, Sharon Freiman and Stephanie Owen, for their assistance.

S. Johnson-Lans (✉)
Vassar College, Poughkeepsie, New York, USA

P. Jones
Oxford University, Oxford, UK

S. Johnson-Lans (ed.), *Wage Inequality in Africa*, Global Perspectives on Wealth and Distribution, DOI 10.1007/978-3-319-51565-6_2

A 10 percent greater ratio of FDI to capital stock in an industrial sector, for example, is associated with about a 1 percent smaller racial wage gap. Moreover, there is evidence that FDI is negatively correlated with market power at the two-digit industry level, thus providing a mechanism that probably enhanced the public policies of that period to reduce racial discrimination, given a Becker-type explanation that reduced market power tends to decrease the level of discrimination that can be engaged in by employers and/or employees.

Keywords Multinationals · FDI · Racial wage gap · South Africa

1 Introduction

Much controversy surrounds the effects of globalization and its impact on labor markets. Opponents of globalization question the long-run benefits of trade reform and relaxed controls, particularly in developing countries although opposition is now rampant in the United States as well. Wages, at least for workers in foreign-owned firms within host countries in the developing world, are usually higher (Aitken et al. 1997; Lipsey 2001; Sjoholm and Lipsey 2006). But there is also evidence that overall wage inequality tends to increase with globalization, at least in earlier stages of development (Figini and Holger 2011). The evolution of wages in Mexico, Colombia, Argentina, Brazil, and Kenya certainly fit this pattern (Cragg and Epelbaum 1996; Hanson and Harrison 1999; Feliciano 2001; Green et al. 2001; Galiani and Sanguinetti 2003; Manda and Sen 2004; Attanasio et al. 2004; Robertson 2004; Waldkirch 2010). Wage inequality also rose in China and India following trade liberalization in the 1990s, sparking even more debate on the short-run benefits of globalization for workers in developing countries (Jian et al. 1996; UNCTAD 2009; Han et al. 2012).

Despite this evidence it is unclear what effect openness to trade and direct foreign investment will have on racial wage inequality in any particular country. The skill premium tends to increase with globalization and thus racially based differences in access to education and skills may result in wider gaps in wages. On the other hand, openness to trade and encouragement of foreign direct investment (FDI) may make markets more competitive, and to the extent that this discourages discrimination, the racial wage gap may tend to narrow.

South Africa is a very interesting country to study because the end of legally sanctioned racial discrimination was accompanied by both pro-labor anti-discriminatory public policy and a dramatic influx of foreign capital into the South African economy.

Studies of wage inequality in South Africa have provided analyses of the racial wage gap, but have tended to focus on the few years during and immediately after the transition to a multi-racial government with the formal end of apartheid. Most studies are limited to cross-sectional examinations of one or a very few years (Atkins and Hinks 1999; Allanson et al. 2000, 2002; Allanson and Atkins 2005; Rospabe 2002; Van Der Berg et al. 2007; Agesa et al. 2010; O'Gorman 2010; Crankshaw 2012; Burger and Jafta 2012[1]; and Ntuli and Kwenda 2014). There is also a remarkable lack of work relating the racial wage gap and foreign investment into South Africa.

We attempt to bridge this gap by analyzing for the first post-apartheid decade the most blatant form of racial wage inequality, namely the difference between black and white wages for workers possessing a given level of human capital, who are in the same occupations and same industries. Thus we attempt to control for both worker characteristics related to productivity and job characteristics, isolating what is usually regarded as a wage gap resulting from either discrimination or unmeasured differences in productivity. One might expect that the first manifestation in the labor market of anti-discrimination policy would be a reduction in this kind of overt wage discrimination, for example, the paying of different wages to workers hired to perform the same jobs within the same industries. Certainly following the Civil Rights legislation of the 1960s in the United States, this form of labor market discrimination was easier to detect and eliminate (or reduce) than more subtle forms of discrimination such as failure to hire or promote, continued occupational segregation, or differences resulting from pre-market discrimination such as differences in access to education and training. To study this form of racial wage discrimination it is necessary to work with individual household and worker-level data and to control for worker and job-related characteristics. We construct a "residual wage gap" that controls for human capital differences, gender, marital status, unionization, type of job, industry, location, and time (year) (Griliches 1969).

The formal end of apartheid was also associated with a resurgence of foreign capital into the South African economy. This happened not only because large foreign firms which had boycotted South Africa (often as a result of shareholder pressure) began to return as investors, but also because public policy in South Africa actively encouraged foreign investment. We therefore investigate the relationship between the extent of FDI in an industry and the racial wage gap. This chapter seeks to enhance our understanding of the effect of this foreign investment on the racial gap in wages in South Africa by addressing two related questions. First, was the foreign investment into South Africa associated with a widening or narrowing of the level of racial wage inequality? And second, what impact, if any, has greater foreign investment had on the degree of market power and concentration in an industry? Both questions are investigated using a two-stage regression strategy and using a merged data set from South Africa which covers the period 1995–2004, thus spanning the country's first decade of democratic rule.

The data include two nationally representative household surveys—the October Household Survey (OHS) and the Labour Force Survey (LFS).[2] Using these surveys, we estimate the average black-white wage gap for each two-digit industry in each year, controlling for relevant worker and job characteristics. The absolute values of these (log) wage gaps are then regressed using a variety of control variables including industry-level measures of FDI in order to estimate the relationship between changes in FDI and changes in the racial wage gap. This estimation strategy is appropriate as long as the differential pattern of foreign investment across sectors is exogenous and labor is not perfectly mobile across industries.

Our results indicate that FDI has been associated with a narrowing of the racial wage gap in South Africa, particularly in the first five post-apartheid years, the period of the presidency of Nelson Mandela. The relationship between the extent of penetration of FDI into an industry and racial wage inequality is both statistically significant and robust across several specifications. Moreover, the impact of FDI on racial inequality is not negligible. A 10 percent rise of the ratio of FDI to capital stock, for example, is associated with about a 1 percent decline in the racial wage gap. This is quite a large effect, given the fact that the ratio of FDI to capital stock doubled between 1995 and 2004.

The greater penetration of foreign capital into certain industries is also found to be associated with an increase in the degree of competition in those industries. This relationship between price-cost margins and FDI is negative, indicating that lower price-cost margins at the industry level (an indication of less market power) are correlated with *higher* levels of FDI.

The outline of the remainder of the chapter is as follows. Section 2 discusses some theoretical explanations about hypothetical links between

FDI and the degree of racial wage inequality. Section 3 describes the data and the method of estimation used in this chapter. Section 4 presents the results from the two-stage estimations. Section 5 summarizes the findings and discusses the implications of them.

2 Foreign Investment and Racial Inequality

There are many different ways in which an individual or firm might hold assets in a foreign country. Whether or not these assets are classified as FDI depends on the definition of foreign investment adopted by a country. According to the South African Reserve Bank (2001, p. S-84), FDI occurs when there is "investment by foreigners in undertakings in South Africa in which they have individually or collectively in the case of affiliated organizations or persons at least 10 percent of the voting rights". Crucial to this definition is the idea that FDI involves some level of control by foreigners of the incorporated or unincorporated enterprise. The South African definition adopts the same "foreign control" criterion which is used by many countries as well as by the International Monetary Fund.[3]

Over the past 20 years many developing countries have actively pursued FDI because of its perceived benefits. These benefits include, inter alia, higher tax revenue from foreign profits, increased wages, and (possibly) external economies in the form of knowledge spillovers. Foreign investment, however, may also affect the host country in ways which are not desirable from a public policy point of view. A large increase in the stock of FDI, for example, could affect the host country's market structure, skill premium, and the level of corporate responsibility which prevails in its business community. These are also channels through which foreign investment may have an impact on the wage differential between black and white workers.

There are several theoretical reasons why globalization might alter the wage distribution across different racial groups. According to the Stolper-Samuelson theorem, countries that are richly endowed with unskilled labor should experience an increase in the return to unskilled labor following trade liberalization. If some races have more skills than others, it follows that trade liberalization will cause distributional changes which favor one race relative to another. As is well known, the Stolper-Samuelson theorem is notoriously difficult to test empirically and most studies which have tested its predictions for developing countries tend to find the opposite effect—that is, trade liberalization causes a widening wage gap between skilled and unskilled workers, not wage convergence. However, as our study abstracts from skill differences and compares workers of different races with the same occupation and experience, this factor would enter in only if there were job segregation that does not show up in the occupational categories available in our data.

Becker's (1957) theory of discrimination offers another channel through which increased trade or capital flows could alter the level of racial inequality within a country. On this theory, increased competition will reduce discrimination, since it will limit the ability of employers (or workers) to indulge their "taste for discrimination". The assumption is that taking into account the psychic cost of having workers of a less favored (racial, ethnic, gender, etc.) group distorts the criterion of hiring and paying workers in accordance with their marginal productivity. Firms with enough market power so that they can mark up prices over costs are therefore more able to engage in discrimination. If foreign investment causes a change in the level of market power and competition in the host country, it could change the level of racial wage inequality in the country as well. To understand the linkages between foreign investment, market structure, and racial inequality, it is therefore important to identify both the potential impact of FDI on the host country's market structure and the impact of market structure on discriminatory behavior (Arrow 1973).

2.1 *Foreign Investment and Market Structure*

Theoretically, greater foreign investment may lead to either an increase or decrease in the level of competition in the host country's product market. The argument linking FDI to greater market concentration is straightforward. It assumes that multinational corporations (MNCs) enter industries where barriers to entry are high. Such entry erodes monopolistic distortions and increases productivity by improving the allocation of resources in the host country. As a result, wages in the host country rise as productivity increases (assuming workers are paid their marginal product). And, racial inequality falls because firms have lower profits and, consequently, less scope to set wages.

Alternatively, foreign investment may reduce the level of competition in the host country. This argument rests on the assumption that local firms find it difficult to compete with MNCs which typically are larger and have access to more sophisticated technologies. Consequently, the entry of MNCs reduces the number of firms in the product market as the least efficient firms (assumed to be local firms) are forced out of business. At the extreme, the entry of a large multinational firm could change the market structure of an industry from a competitive market to a monopoly. Given this scenario, it is likely that racial wage inequality would rise because the monopoly would have higher profits and, consequently, more scope to discriminate. This, of course, assumes that legal prohibitions on racial discrimination are not completely enforced.

On the other hand, consumer pressure on multinationals to practice "fair" trade and implement international labor standards may create an economic incentive for MNCs to improve the working conditions of disadvantaged workers in developing countries. In recent years, activists have worked hard to put labor rights on the global agenda. These efforts have had some limited success in changing corporate behavior with respect to human rights, worker rights, and environmental protection (Elliott and Freeman 2001). Indeed, South Africa was one of the first countries to successfully use grass-roots activism to improve working conditions and change corporate policies toward the advancement of black workers. If MNCs respond to consumer pressure by adopting policies that favor disadvantaged workers, racial wage inequality should fall.

3 Data and Estimation Techniques

This study employs an unusually rich data set to investigate the impact of FDI on racial wage inequality in South Africa. Data are drawn from 10 years of two nationally representative household surveys: (1) the OHS (1995–1999) and (2) the LFS (2000–2004). Each year between 1995 and 2001 represents an independent cross section of the South African population, as different samples were designed for each survey. In 2000, however, the OHS was replaced by the LFS, a rotating panel that was conducted biannually.[4] Starting in March 2001, 20 percent of the households in the LFS were rotated out every six months. While it would be preferable for the purposes of this study to have independent cross sections for each year, the estimates obtained from regression analysis using the 2002–2004 data are still unbiased and therefore should not affect the accuracy of our results.

Both surveys have nationally representative samples and contain information on individuals' wages, industry, occupation, region of residence, and various demographic characteristics such as gender, race, age, and education. The OHS was administered by Statistics South Africa and originally funded by the Governments of Denmark, the Netherlands, and Norway working through the World Bank. The survey collected extensive data on workers employed in both the formal and informal sectors of the economy. All workers aged 15 and above were asked to report their wage as an absolute value or within an income range, as well as the number of hours worked per week. A majority of workers (approximately 70 percent) reported a specific value for their wage. For those who chose an income category, the logarithmic mean of the two end points of the indicated income range was taken as their estimated wage. All wages reflect gross values as the survey asked workers to report the value of their wages, including overtime, allowances, and bonuses before any tax deductions.

The sample used for analysis includes all black and white workers aged 15–65 who either worked 20 or more hours during the last seven days or were absent from work but still had a job (i.e., workers on holiday, sick leave, etc.). Since blacks have suffered the highest degree of discrimination in South Africa, and whites the least, this study compares and contrasts only the two extremes: black and white workers. Therefore, colored and Asians are omitted from the samples used. Workers employed by exterior organizations and foreign governments and those with activities not adequately defined were deleted from the sample. In addition, workers employed in the utilities sector were deleted. The number of workers who were interviewed by the OHS and employed in the utilities sector was very small in any given year; the number ranged from 128 workers in 1998 (out of a total sample of 9,931 workers) to 261 workers in 1994 (out of a total sample of 18,110 workers). To check whether the elimination of these workers affected the results, we estimated two linear regressions—one with workers from the utility sector and one without. The results were not significantly different.

In South Africa large differences exist between black and white workers. The descriptive statistics in Table A.1 illustrate some of these differences by reporting a set of statistics for both black and white workers calculated using the 1995 OHS and the 2004 LFS. Not surprisingly, the (gross) wage differential between the two racial groups is very large. White workers earned, on average, 33 rand per week in 2004 which is three times larger than the hourly wages of black workers (11 rand). Much of this wage differential is explained by differences in human capital accumulation and occupation. White workers have on average 13 years of education versus 9 years for blacks.[5] And a larger proportion of white workers are employed in skilled occupations. Thirteen percent of all whites are employed in management positions versus only 1 percent of blacks. Similarly, 15 percent of all whites are employed in professional occupations versus only 2 percent of blacks.

The worker data were supplemented with annual data at the two-digit industry level on FDI and fixed capital stock. The information on FDI and capital stock was collected by the South African Reserve Bank and published in various years of the *Quarterly Bulletin of Statistics*. For the purposes of this study, FDI is defined as the ratio of the stock of foreign investment to gross capital stock in each economic sector at the two-digit level. We use a stock measure rather than a flow measure because discriminatory behavior is more likely related to the relative dominance of MNCs in the economic sector in which they operate at a point in time. Both FDI and gross capital stock are measured in millions of rand and deflated to 2000 values. The FDI measure varies by year and sector which permits the inclusion of both industry and year fixed effects in the regressions. The advantage of using both sets of fixed effects is that they should capture unobserved differences across both industries and time.

To determine the importance of foreign investment on racial inequality, we use a two-stage estimation process. First, a wage equation is estimated for workers in each two-digit industry, controlling for human capital factors, personal characteristics, region, occupation, industry, unionization, and racial group. The wage equation is specified as follows:

$$\log W_{ij} = \alpha + \underline{X}_i \beta + \underline{Z}_j \gamma + \varepsilon_{ij} \qquad (1)$$

where

W_{ij} is the weekly wage of worker i who belongs to racial group j,
$\underline{X}_i$ is the vector of personal characteristics, region, occupation, and union status for worker i,
$\underline{Z}_j$ is the vector of mutually exclusive dummy variables indicating racial group j,
ε_{ij} is the random disturbance term,

and α is the intercept term, and β and γ are the parameter vectors. The racial fixed effect, γ, represents the (industry and year specific) average wage gap between black and white workers, controlling for personal and industry attributes. Separate regressions are estimated for each industry and year.[6]

Controls for personal characteristics include gender, marital status, years of education, years of job experience and its square, occupation, and average hours worked per week. Workers are assigned 1 year of education up to 17 years. Job experience is estimated in the usual manner as age minus years of education minus six. In addition, the regression includes eight occupation controls,[7] eight region controls,[8] a dummy variable for rural residence, and a dummy variable for union status.

It is hypothesized that the racial wage gap in each economic sector is associated with the concentration of FDI in that sector. To test this hypothesis, we estimate the following regression in which the wage gap depends on the sector-specific ratio of FDI to capital stock and on an additional set of sector-specific variables. That is,

$$\log \gamma_{jk} = \mu + Q_{jk}\lambda + \rho_j + \phi_k + \nu_{jk} \tag{2}$$

where

γ_{jk} is the racial (absolute) wage differential for industry j in year k,
Q_{jk} is the level of FDI for industry j in year k,
ν_{jk} is the random disturbance term,

and μ is the intercept term, ρ_j are industry fixed effects, ϕ_k are year fixed effects, and λ is the parameter estimate on FDI. The coefficient on the ratio of FDI to capital stock, λ, estimates the importance of foreign investment on the wage gap. A positive sign on the FDI coefficient would indicate that an increase in the ratio of FDI to capital stock is associated with greater racial inequality, for example, with an increase in the wage gap. Similarly, a negative coefficient indicates that a rise in the ratio of FDI to capital stock is associated with less racial wage inequality. Both results are consistent with economic theories outlined earlier in the chapter.

Although the wage equations control for individual differences in labor quality, industry differences may exist as well. Some industries, for example, may simply attract "higher quality" workers. Such industry differences may affect the level of racial wage inequality if "quality" differences exist across different racial groups. To control for these differences, we include several sector-specific variables when estimating Equation (2). Industry-specific controls for human capital (i.e., average years of education and average years of experience) are included to control for labor "quality" differences across industries. The proportion of unionized workers is included because unionized sectors generally pay higher wages. The proportion of black workers in an industry also may be related to the wage gap, although no assumption is made about whether it is likely to augment or reduce the magnitude of the gap. Lastly, capital intensity is included as it may affect the return to skill.

4 Estimation Results

Table A.2 presents the black-white wage gaps estimated from the wage equations for all workers in each of the nine major economic sectors. For the average black worker, the wage gap worsened over the period 1995–2004. In 1994 black workers earned, on average, 61 percent less than white workers, controlling for gender, education, work experience, hours worked per week, rural residence, location, occupation, and union status. By 2004 this wage gap had risen to 71 percent, although it varied somewhat in the interim years. One reason for this, outside the scope of this study, may have been the continuing, and even increasing, high level of unemployment, particularly among blacks. Table A.3 shows the wage gaps for male workers. Note that the gaps are generally larger when female workers are excluded.

The data indicate that there were also large differences in the racial wage gap across economic sectors. For most years, black workers employed in agriculture, construction, and mining were the worst paid relative to white workers. By contrast, black workers were relatively well paid in the service and financial sectors. Similar results are reported in Table A.3 which lists the estimated wage gaps for the sample of males only.

In the second-stage regressions, the absolute values of the log racial wage gaps (see Tables A.2 and A.3) are regressed on the logarithm of two measures of FDI and several industry-specific variables.[9] This two-stage estimation process is used as a way to get around the aggregation problem which results from the correlations between the characteristics of individual workers and the deviations of their firm's characteristics from the average characteristics of their industry. Dickens and Ross (1984) suggest a two-stage estimation procedure as a solution to the aggregation problem [10]

Table A.4 presents the second-stage regression results for the years 1995–2004 using the absolute value of the black-white wage gap as the dependent variables. Three time periods are analyzed: (1) the period 1995–1999 which coincides with the Mandela years of government; (2)

the period 2000–2004 which coincides with the first five years of Mbeki's presidency; and (3) the period 1995–2004.[11] For the Mandela years the coefficient on FDI is negative and significant, indicating that sectors with a greater concentration of foreign capital exhibited a lower racial wage gap.

But what has led to this narrowing of the racial wage gap? As discussed earlier in the paper, there are possible theoretical links between globalization and the racial wage gap. Becker's theory, for example, predicts that discrimination is linked to the level of competition in the economy. If FDI affects the level of competition, it follows that FDI could affect the level of racial wage inequality. To determine the effect of FDI on the level of competition, we regress the ratio of FDI to capital stock on price-cost margins at the two-digit industry level, controlling for year fixed effects. The results from this regression are reported in Table A.5. The results indicate that there is a strong link between the ratio of FDI to capital stock at the two-digit industry levels and price-cost margins. This relationship is negative, indicating that greater price-cost margins at the industry level are correlated with *lower* levels of FDI. This finding provides empirical support for the fact that the lower racial wage gap in industries having a higher degree of FDI penetration may be being driven, at least in part, by changes in the level of competition at the two-digit industry level associated with degree of penetration of FDI into an industry.[12]

It is also interesting to note (See Table A.4) that the effect of unions seems to be to increase the racial differential in wages, at least in the first five years of the period studied. And for the second 5-year period in the decade, the racial wage gap is lower in industries in which workers are, on average, more educated. This suggests that increasing returns to education for black workers may have begun to appear in the later part of the period studied. It is also interesting to note that the magnitude of the effects on racial wage differentials of FDI penetration into an industry and of unionization are greater for male than for all workers, implying that the female racial wage gap may be less affected by foreign investment and that the racial wage gap between unionized and non-unionized women may also be less pronounced.

5 Conclusion

The results presented in this chapter provide some evidence that the gap between wages of black and white workers in South Africa is lower in industry sectors with increased multinational activity, at least during the first five post-apartheid years. Using a two-stage estimation process, which controls for differences in human capital across individuals and for occupational and industry differences, we find that higher levels in the ratio of FDI to capital stock are associated with lower levels of racial wage inequality. A 10 percent increase in the ratio of FDI to capital stock, for example, is associated with about a 1 percent decrease in the black-white wage gap. In addition, the chapter examines the extent to which FDI is associated with the level of competition in the host country, South Africa. The results show that greater FDI penetration into an industry is associated with lower price-cost margins and hence with (probable) greater degrees of competition. This provides an explanation for the finding that the racial wage gap is lower in sectors with higher proportions of FDI to capital stock.

The empirical work in this chapter attempts to measure only the most overt form of racial labor market discrimination, namely, pay differences for workers in the same occupation who are equal with respect to years of education, experience, and unionization, and are employed in the same industries. In spite of anti-discrimination labor law, the gap is, however, still significant. In fact, there is independent evidence that the South African racial wage gap did not decrease with the enactment of the anti-discrimination legislation. According to Allanson and Atkins, the unexplained portion of the overall racial wage differential actually increased over the period 1993–1999 (Allanson and Atlkins 2005).

There are many questions remaining. For instance, what about differential unemployment rates between the races? What about racial differences in access to unionized jobs and in pay differentials in unionized versus non-unionized jobs? And, what about racial differences in returns to education? It is important to take account of the fact that in the post-apartheid period South Africa appears to have experienced a worsening in the state of the labor market, with the unemployment rates increasing as capital-intensive industry gained ground over labor-intensive sectors. The emphasis on economic growth, focusing on promoting capital intensive industry, was conscious government policy. The African National Union (ANU) government, in power since 1994, had a main macroeconomic policy aim from 1996 on known as GEAR (Growth, Employment, and Redistribution).[13] This was certainly not unambiguously labor friendly in that it aimed to improve the country's international competitiveness by "attracting foreign capital, cutting budget deficits and restraining wages" (Jenkins 2006, 662). With double-digit unemployment rates persisting at an average rate of about 25 percent up to the present decade (Bhorat et al. 2014), minor improvements in the relative wage position of those fortunate enough to have jobs does not necessarily signify a net improvement in the lives of South African workers, and certainly not in the lives of black South African workers (Azam and Rospabe 1999).

Black unemployment rates have been dramatically higher than those for white workers throughout the entire period (Jenkins 2008). Governmental affirmative action policies were found to have had little if any effect on the overall racial gap in employment opportunities (Burger and Jafta 2012). For instance, the upper limit estimate of the White-African employment gap ratio increased from 12 to 17.4 percent between 1995 and 2002 (Brookes and Hinks 2004). And using OECD data, for the (narrower) *official* definition of unemployment,[14] African (black) unemployment rates for 1993, 1997, 2001, and 2005 were 17, 27.1, 35.1, and 31.1 percent, respectively, compared with those for whites of 3.2, 3.9, 5.6, and 4.9 percent (Leibbrandt et al. 2010, from Table 1.8).

The question of the effect of unions on racial wage differentials is a complex one (Bhorat et al. 2012). The early Mandela years featured policies that promoted unionization. These became greatly watered down in the later part of the period studied. But how did unionization in fact affect racial wage discrimination? Studies disagree. Casale and Posel found that unionization tended to compress the black/white male wage differential (Casel and Posel 2011). On the other hand, Ntuli and Kwenda found that the net effect of unionization for African males appears to have increased racial wage inequality (Ntuli and Kwenda 2014). Our regression results similarly find that the effect of unionization was to widen the racial wage gap during the period 1995–1999. It is significant for all workers and significant at a $p = 0.10$ level for the subset of males. However, the union effect on the racial wage gap was no longer significant in the period 2000–2004. It is possible that anti-discrimination policy directed toward unions began to take effect in the later period or simply that union power declined.

With respect to returns to education, a study covering the same period as the one we have analyzed found no strong downward trend in wage discrimination of the kind that we have estimated. It did, however, point to the increased importance of returns to education resulting in a narrowing of the racial wage gap at the top of the wage distribution. The implication is that affirmative action policies of the South African government toward improving the quality of black education have primarily affected the top end of the occupational ladder (Burger and Jafta 2012). Our results for the period 2000–2004 are consistent with this finding since the racial wage gap was found to be significantly lower (both for all workers and for males) in industries where average years of education of workers is higher

Thus it appears that the modest beginnings in improving the relative position of *employed* black workers in South Africa during the Mandela years were only that (Allanson et al. 2002). High unemployment and much higher unemployment among blacks than among whites has remained a major problem until the present time. Moreover, the persistent racial inequality in access to education and in quality of education means that blacks are still predominately located in the lower-skilled occupations which are much more vulnerable to unemployment, given globalization and rapid changes in technology, both of which favor skilled over unskilled workers (Bjerk 2007).

In conclusion, we found some evidence of a negative association between degree of foreign investment in an industry and the size of racial wage differentials and of a positive association between foreign investment and competitiveness of markets. This lends no support to the notion that globalization promotes labor market discrimination. We also found some evidence suggesting that over time South African unions may be becoming less racially discriminatory and that by the second half of the decade black workers may have been doing relatively better when employed in industry sectors that hire more highly educated workers.

Table A.1 Descriptive statistics of black and white workers in 1995 and 2004

	Black workers		White workers	
	1995	2004	1995	2004
Personal characteristics				
Hourly wage	6.82	10.9	21.8	32.9
Male	0.69	0.65	0.58	0.52
Married	0.54	0.53	0.74	0.70
Years of education	5.91	9.1	10.2	12.5
Years of work experience	25.7	22.2	21.1	19.6
Hours worked per week	45.6	48.0	45.1	44.6
Union	0.34	0.32	0.24	0.33
Manager	0.01	0.01	0.10	0.13
Professional	0.02	0.02	0.08	0.07
Technician	0.10	0.09	0.20	0.18
Clerks	0.08	0.07	0.26	0.26
Sales	0.12	0.14	0.13	0.13
Skilled agriculture	0.01	0.01	0.02	0.00
Artisan	0.10	0.15	0.15	0.13
Operator	0.16	0.16	0.05	0.05
Unskilled	0.40	0.34	0.02	0.04
Industry characteristics				
Agriculture	0.26	0.19	0.03	0.04
Mining	0.07	0.07	0.06	0.05
Manufacturing	0.14	0.15	0.15	0.14
Construction	0.05	0.09	0.03	0.02
Trade	0.14	0.17	0.20	0.22
Transport	0.04	0.04	0.08	0.05
Finance	0.03	0.07	0.14	0.16
Services	0.27	0.23	0.30	0.32
Regional characteristics				
Western Cape	0.04	0.05	0.15	0.21
Eastern Cape	0.15	0.11	0.11	0.10
Northern Cape	0.02	0.04	0.04	0.11
Free State	0.15	0.11	0.10	0.10
KwaZulu Natal	0.20	0.26	0.14	0.12
North West	0.11	0.10	0.07	0.06
Guateng	0.16	0.15	0.30	0.19
Mpumalanga	0.12	0.11	0.06	0.07
Northern Province	0.04	0.08	0.03	0.05
Number of observations	10,966	8,257	3,246	794

Source: 1995 OHS and 2004 LFS (September).

Table A.2 Black-white wage gaps for all workers, 1995–2004

	1995	*1996*	*1997*	*1998*	*1999*	*2000*	*2001*	*2002*	*2003*	*2004*
Agriculture, forestry, and fishing	-1.034	-1.421	-0.888	-0.844	-1.089	-1.329	-1.208	0.431	-1.145	-1.143
	(0.118)	(0.184)	(0.146)	(0.233)	(0.107)	(0.142)	(0.177)	(0.260)	(0.176)	(0.264)
	[2,947]	[803]	[1,666]	[1,294]	[1,862]	[1,641]	[1,526]	[1,668]	[1,538]	[1,611]
Mining and quarrying	-0.966	-0.781	-0.900	-0.826	-1.131	-1.024	-1.083	-0.875	-0.935	-0.896
	(0.054)	(0.106)	(0.071)	(0.119)	(0.124)	(0.069)	(0.072)	(0.092)	(0.090)	(0.144)
	[977]	[364]	[364]	[753]	[1,177]	[1,216]	[1,116]	[1,034]	[1,061]	[577]
Manufacturing	-0.728	-0.802	-0.851	-0.844	-0.796	-1.002	-0.960	-0.806	-0.953	-0.801
	(0.042)	(0.066)	(0.047)	(0.065)	(0.068)	(0.065)	(0.060)	(0.073)	(0.072)	(0.108)
	[1,990]	[1,354]	[2,538]	[1,222]	[1,653]	[1,752]	[1,561]	[1,329]	[1,204]	[1,362]
Construction	-1.037	-0.763	-0.856	-0.923	-0.842	-1.159	-0.688	-0.634	-0.952	-0.982
	(0.090)	(0.198)	(0.107)	(0.172)	(0.332)	(0.175)	(0.126)	(0.165)	(0.196)	(0.201)
	[635]	[457]	[823]	[509]	[635]	[792]	[627]	[530]	[529]	[746]
Wholesale and retail trade, catering, and Accommodation	-0.608	-0.859	-0.723	-0.704	-0.784	-0.910	-0.805	-0.760	-0.840	-0.748
	(0.038)	(0.076)	(0.049)	(0.062)	(0.066)	(0.063)	(0.060)	(0.070)	(0.060)	(0.060)
	[2,166]	[1,241]	[2,229]	[1,383]	[1,910]	[1,866]	[1,665]	[1,362]	[1,424]	[1,564]
Transport, storage, and communication	-0.632	-0.480	-0.894	-0.720	-0.695	-0.589	-0.844	-0.808	-0.537	-0.543
	(0.051)	(0.100)	(0.065)	(0.092)	(0.088)	(0.083)	(0.095)	(0.103)	(0.116)	(0.122)
	[740]	[494]	[874]	[500]	[588]	[606]	[530]	[455]	[413]	[402]
Finance, insurance, real estate, and business services	-0.423	-0.400	-0.712	-0.442	-0.540	-0.662	-0.620	-0.597	-0.596	-0.731
	(0.049)	(0.077)	(0.061)	(0.080)	(0.086)	(0.075)	(0.091)	(0.080)	(0.083)	(0.094)
	[803]	[697]	[1,038]	[634]	[995]	[898]	[750]	[688]	[648]	[663]
Community, social, and personal services	-0.441	-0.3862	-0.523	-0.497	-0.420	-0.378	-0.461	-0.474	-0.381	-0.508
	(0.024)	(0.044)	(0.035)	(0.047)	(0.047)	(0.040)	(0.042)	(0.055)	(0.057)	(0.066)
	[3,954]	[2,388]	[5,698]	[3,212]	[2,905]	[2,673]	[2,277]	[1,934]	[1,870]	[2,126]

(*continued*)

Table A.2 (continued)

	1995	*1996*	*1997*	*1998*	*1999*	*2000*	*2001*	*2002*	*2003*	*2004*
All sectors[a]	−0.606	−0.606	−0.703	−0.648	−0.667	−0.719	−0.738	−0.650	−0.704	−0.713
	(0.020)	(0.027)	(0.020)	(0.027)	(0.028)	(0.025)	(0.026)	(0.029)	(0.031)	(0.034)
	[14,212]	[7,795]	[15,790]	[9, 507]	[11,725]	[11,444]	[10,052]	[9,000]	[8,687]	[9,051]

Notes: Author's regressions using the October Household Surveys (1994–1999) and Labour Force Surveys (2000–2006). Dependent variable is the log of hourly wages. Controls include race dummy, gender dummy, years of education, work experience and its square, average hours worked per week, rural dummy, eight region dummies, eight occupation dummies, and union dummy. Regressions are weighted by population weights as described in text. Standard errors reported in parentheses.

[a]Regressions exclude workers employed by extra-territorial organizations or foreign governments, as well as workers in unspecified or unclassified sectors and occupations. Sample size of each regression reported in brackets. Sample includes all black and white workers who work 20+ hours per week.

Table A.3 Black-white wage gaps for males only, 1995–2004

	1995	*1996*	*1997*	*1998*	*1999*	*2000*	*2001*	*2002*	*2003*	*2004*
Agriculture,	-1.022	-1.536	-0.779	-0.842	-1.01	-1.586	-1.270	-0.355	-1.121	-1.690
forestry, and fishing	(0.136)	(0.204)	(0.150)	(0.256)	(0.126)	(0.140)	(0.208)	(0.266)	(0.226)	(0.286)
	[2,416]	[606]	[1,129]	[945]	[1,254]	[1,116]	[1,129]	[1,186]	[1,123]	[1,170]
Mining and	-1.020	-0.823	-0.913	-0.804	-1.067	-1.010	-1.134	-0.830	-1.014	-0.906
quarrying	(0.055)	(0.110)	(0.077)	(0.127)	(0.090)	(0.072)	(0.072)	(0.098)	(0.094)	(0.156)
	[925]	[340]	[868]	[725]	[1,126]	[1,179]	[1,083]	[1,000]	[1,026]	[554]
Manufacturing	-0.748	-0.787	-0.840	-0.782	-0.768	-0.992	-1.012	-0.8198	-0.894	-0.732
	(0.050)	(0.075)	(0.054)	(0.082)	(0.078)	(0.079)	(0.071)	(0.089)	(0.083)	(0.124)
	[1,404]	[942]	[1,785]	[821]	[1,132]	[1,180]	[1,033]	[878]	[814]	[843]
Construction	-1.072	-0.731	-0.879	-0.935	-0.778	-1.1883	-0.670	-0.739	-0.888	-1.032
	(0.092)	(0.210)	(0.114)	(0.192)	(0.074)	(0.190)	(0.129)	(0.165)	(0.207)	(0.221)
	[600]	[426]	[757]	[482]	[1,005]	[743]	[571]	[488]	[467]	[661]
Wholesale and retail	-0.7400	-0.982	-0.741	-0.739	-0.835	-1.009	-0.867	-0.767	-0.944	-0.742
trade, catering, and	(0.057)	(0.107)	(0.062)	(0.084)	(0.074)	(0.099)	(0.090)	(0.095)	(0.097)	(0.075)
accommodation	[1,145]	[660]	[1,205]	[746]	[1,005]	[1,024]	[904]	[729]	[767]	[842]
Transport, storage,	-0.697	-0.568	-0.890	-0.873	-0.734	-0.685	-0.809	-0.896	-0.531	-0.523
and communication	(0.057)	(0.114)	(0.071)	(0.110)	(0.084)	(0.091)	(0.105)	(0.119)	(0.144)	(0.157)
	[407]	[433]	[738]	[410]	[494]	[529]	[447]	[377]	[343]	[340]
Finance, insurance,	-0.565	-0.479	-0.860	-0.346	-0.760	-0.763	-0.741	-0.650	-0.594	-0.861
real estate, and	(0.069)	(0.108)	(0.084)	(0.108)	(0.138)	(0.123)	(0.129)	(0.105)	(0.117)	(0.137)
business services	[803]	[417]	[622]	[391]	[549]	[529]	[425]	[432]	[413]	[437]
Community, social,	-0.441	-0.531	-0.576	-0.624	-0.528	-0.464	-0.503	-0.488	-0.453	-0.465
and personal	(0.024)	(0.068)	(0.055)	(0.070)	(0.063)	(0.064)	(0.069)	(0.094)	(0.083)	(0.104)
services	[3,954]	[1,084]	[2,043]	[1,086]	[1,312]	[1,151]	[999]	[835]	[839]	[904]
All sectors[a]	**-0.733**	**-0.717**	**-0.769**	**-0.682**	**-0.7688**	**-0.862**	**-0.844**	**-0.698**	**-0.802**	**-0.747**
	(0.020)	(0.036)	(0.025)	(0.037)	(0.035)	(0.035)	(0.035)	(0.039)	(0.040)	(0.048)
	[9,470]	[4,908]	[9,147]	[5,606]	[7,450]	[7,451]	[6,591]	[5,925]	[5,799]	[5,751]

Notes: Same as Table A.2.

Table A.4 FDI and racial wage inequality

Dependent variable: ln[black white wage gap]	*Mandela years: 1995–1999*		*Mbeki years: 2000–2004*		*First decade of ANC rule: 1995–2004*	
	All workers (1)	*Males only* (2)	*All workers* (3)	*Males only* (4)	*All workers* (5)	*Males only* (6)
ln(FDI/K)	–0.116**	–0.146**	0.112	0.114	–0.064*	–0.073**
	(0.049)	(0.054)	(0.100)	(0.107)	(0.034)	(0.036)
ln(K/L)	0.311	0.531*	0.081	0.150	0.108	0.173
	(0.268)	(0.287)	(0.079)	(0.111)	(0.145)	(0.190)
ln(proportion unionized)	0.560**	0.832*	-0.255	-0.281	0.082	0.235
	(0.320)	(0.320)	(0.494)	(0.675)	(0.183)	(0.235)
ln(proportion black)	0.448	0.386	-1.081	-0.970	-0.347	-0.049
	(0.769)	(0.769)	(1.042)	(1.28)	(0.388)	(0.447)
ln(avg. years of education)	-0.334	-1.336	-0.855**	-1.039*	-0.203	-0.251
	(0.948)	(0.956)	(0.3855)	(0.526)	(0.253)	(0.284)
ln(avg. years of experience)	-0.944	-1.353	-2.341	-3.124	-0.336	-0.518
	(0.944)	(1.076)	(2.020)	(2.229)	(0.493)	(0.502)
Industry fixed effects	Yes	Yes	Yes	Yes	Yes	Yes
Year fixed effects	Yes	Yes	Yes	Yes	Yes	Yes
Observations	40	40	40	40	80	80
R^2	0.8827	0.7428	0.8131	0.7485	0.7253	0.5587

Notes: Robust standard errors are reported in parentheses; ** denotes value significance at the 1% level, * denotes value significance at the 5% level.

Table A.5 FDI and price-cost margins

Logarithm(FDI/K)	−0.840**
	(0.128)
Industry characteristics	No
Industry fixed effects	No
Year fixed effects	Yes
Observations	49
R^2	0.5031

Notes: Price-cost margins calculated for mining, manufacturing, construction, trade, and transportation sectors **denotes value significance at the 1% level.

Notes

1. One notable exception is a 2012 paper of Burger and Jafta, which is discussed in the final section of this chapter.
2. The October Household Survey (OHS; Statistics South Africa 1995–1999) was conducted each year from 1995 to 1999. The Labour Force Survey (LFS) replaced the OHS in 2000 and was conducted biannually from 2001 to 2007.
3. See Lipsey (2001) for a good discussion of how the concept and measurement of FDI has changed over time.
4. A pilot survey was conducted in 2000 in which a new sample was drawn. In 2001 a new sample was drawn as well. The 2001 households become the base sample for the rotating panel.
5. Evidence suggests that the quality of education received by blacks was much lower too (see Case and Deaton 1999).
6. The eight industries used for analysis are (1) agriculture, forestry, and fishing; (2) mining and quarrying; (3) manufacturing; (4) construction; (5) wholesale and retail trade, catering, and accommodation; (6) transport, storage, and communication; (7) finance, insurance, real estate, and business services; and (8) community, social, and personal services.
7. The occupational controls are manager, professionals, semi-professionals and technicians, clerks, salespersons and skilled service workers, skilled agricultural workers, and artisans. Unskilled routine operators are the omitted occupational dummy.
8. The regional controls are Western Cape, Eastern Cape, Northern Cape, Free State, Guateng, North West, Mpumalanga, and Northern Province. KwaZulu-Natal is the omitted regional dummy.
9. The absolute value of the black-white wage gap can be used because all values are negative.

10. This estimation is appropriate as long as the differential pattern of foreign investment across sectors is exogenous and labor is not perfectly mobile across sectors. Both assumptions are plausible in the short run.
11. Nelson Mandela was elected president of South Africa on April 27, 1994, and stayed in power until June 1999 when Thabo Mbeki took office. Mbeki remained in office until September 2008.
12. It is well known that the quality of schooling in South Africa has been lower for blacks than for whites. We have no evidence of a selection bias problem affecting our results. However, if there were unmeasured racial differences in quality of human capital that varied systematically between workers employed in the industrial sectors with higher and lower levels of FDI penetration, then the lower racial wage gap might also be reflecting this. This is an important area for future research.
13. The ANU is the government that was formed in 1994; and dominant party from this period to the present time has been the African National Congress (ANC).
14. Statistics South Africa uses the following definition of unemployment as its "official" definition: Those people within the economically active population who (a) did not work during the seven days prior to the interview, (b) want to work and are available to start working within a week, and (c) have taken active steps to look for work or to start some form of self-employment in the four weeks prior to the interview. The "expanded unemployment rate", also frequently used, omits (c).

References

Agesa, Richard, Jacqueline Agesa, and Geoffrey Bongani. 2010. "Higher Residual Wage Dispersion for White Workers in Post-Apartheid South Africa, 1995–2006: Compositional Effects or Higher Skill Prices?" *Journal of Developing Areas* 44(1): 71–100.

Aitken, Brian, Ann Harrison, and Robert E. Lipsey. 1997. "Wages and Foreign Ownership: A Comparative Study of Mexico, Venezuela, and the United States," *Journal of International Economics* 40: 345–371.

Allanson, Paul et al. 2002. "No End to the Racial Wage Hierarchy in South Africa?," *Review of Development Economics* 6(3): 442–459.

Allanson, Paul, and Jonathan P. Atkins. 2005. "The Evolution of the Racial Wage Hierarchy in Post-Apartheid South Africa," *Journal of Development Studies* 41(6): 1023–1050.

Allanson, Paul, Jonathan P. Atkins, and Timothy Hinks. 2000. "A Multilateral Decomposition of Racial Wage Differentials in the 1994 South African Labour Market," *Journal of Development Studies* 37(1): 93–120.

Arrow, Kenneth. 1973. "The Theory of Discrimination," in *Discrimination in Labor Markets*, Orley Ashenfelter and Albert Rees, eds., Princeton: Princeton University Press.

Atkins, Jonathan P., and Timothy Hinks. 1999. "The Economics of Racial Discrimination in the Labour Marketr," *Post-Beckerian Theory and Estimation Procedures with Applications to South Africa, the Current State of Economic Science* 4: 2035–2054.

Attanasio, Orazio, Pinelopi Koujianou Goldberg, and Nina Pavcnik. 2004. "Trade Reforms and Wage Inequality in Colombia," *Journal of Development Economics* 74(2): 221–366.

Azam, J.-P., and S. Rospabe. 1999. "Trade Unions and Statistical Discrimination. Theory with Reference to South Africa," Paper presented at annual conference of the European Economic Association, Santiago de Compostela, September, 1999.

Becker, Gary. 1957. *The Economics of Discrimination*. Chicago: University of Chicago Press.

Bhorat, Haroon, et al. 2012. "Institutional Wage Effects: Revisiting Union and Bargaining Council Wage Premia in South Africa," *South African Journal of Economics* 80(3): 400–414.

Bhorat, Haroon, et al. 2014. "Trade Unions in an Emerging Economy," United Nations University (UNU-WIDER) Working Paper 2014/55.

Bjerk, David. 2007. "The Differential Effects of Black White Wage Inequality Across Employment Sectors," *Journal of Human Resources* 42(2): 398–437.

Brookes, Michael, and Timothy Hinks. 2004. "The Racial Employment Gap in South Africa," *South African Journal of Economics* 72(3): 573–597.

Burger, Rulof, and Rachel Jafta. 2012. "Returns to Race: Labor Market Discrimination in Post-Apartheid South Africa," *Development South Africa* 29: 5.

Casale, D., and D. Posel. 2011. "Unions and the Gender Wage Gap in South Africa," *Journal of African Economics* 10(1): 27–59.

Case, Anne, and Angus Deaton. 1999. "School Inputs and Educational Outcomes in South Africa," *Quarterly Journal of Economics* 114(3): 1047–1084.

Cragg, Michael Ian, and Mario Epelbaum. 1996. "Why Has Wage Dispersion Grown in Mexico? Is It the Incidence of Reforms or the Growing Demand for Skills?" *Journal of Development Economics* 51: 99–116.

Crankshaw, Owen. 2012. "Deindustrialization, Professionalism, and Racial Inequality in Capetown," *Urban Affairs* 48(6): 836–862.

Dickens, William T., and B. Ross. 1984. "Consistent Estimation Using Data From More than One Sample," NBER Technical Working Paper No. 33, National Bureau of Economic Research, Cambridge, MA.

Elliott, Kimberly Ann, and Richard B. Freeman. 2001. "White Hats or Don Quixotes? Human Rights Vigilantes in the Global Economy." NBER Working Paper 8102. National Bureau of Economic Research, Cambridge Mass. (January).

Feliciano, Zadia. 2001. "Workers and Trade Liberalization: The Impact of Trade Reforms in Mexico on Wages and Employment," *Industrial and Labor Relations Review* 55(1): 95–115.

Figini, Paolo, and Holger Gorg. 2011. "Does Foreign Direct Investment Affect Wage Inequality? An Empirical Investigation," *The World Economy* 34(9): 1455–1474.

Galiani, Sebastian, and Pablo Sanguinetti. 2003. "The Impact of Trade Liberalization on Wage Inequality: Evidence From Argentina," *Journal of Development Economics* 72(2): 497–513.

Green, Francis, Andy Dickerson, and Jorge Saba Arbache. 2001. "A Picture of Wage Inequality and the Allocation of Labor Through a Period of Liberalization: The Case of Brazil," *World Development* 29(11): 1923–1939.

Griliches, Zvi. 1969. "Capital-Skill Complementarity," *Review of Economics and Statistics* 51(4): 465–470.

Han, Jun, Liu Runjuan, and Junsen Zhang. 2012. "Global and Wage Inequality: Evidence from Urban China," *Journal of International Economics* 87(2): 836–862.

Hanson, Gordon, and Ann Harrison. 1999. "Who Gains From Trade Reform? Some Remaining Puzzles?" *Journal of Development Economics* 59: 125–154.

Jenkins, Rhys. 2006. "Globalization and the Labour Market in South Africa," *Journal of International Development* 18: 649–664.

Jenkins, Rhys. 2008. "Trade, Technology, and Employment in South Africa," *Journal of Development Studies* 44(1): 60–79.

Juin, Tianlun, Jeffrey D. Sachs, and Andrew M. Warner. 1996. "Trends in Regional Inequality in China," *China Economic Review* 7: 1.

Leibbrandt, Murray et al. 2010. *Employment and Inequality Outcomes in South Africa*, South Africa Labor and Development Research Unite (SALDRU) and School of Economics, University of Cape Town. www.oecd.org/employment/emp45282868.pdf.

Lipsey, Robert E. 2001. "Foreign Direct Investment and the Operations of Multinational Firms: Concepts, History, and Data." NBER Working Paper 8665. National Bureau of Economic Research, Cambridge, MA (December).

Manda, Damiano Kulundu, and Kunal Sen. 2004. "The Labour Market Effects of Globalization in Kenya," *Journal of International Development* 16: 29–43.

Ntuli, M., and P. Kwenda. 2014. " Labour Unions and Wage Inequality Among African Men in South Africa," *Development South Africa* 31(2): 322–346.

O'Gorman, Melanie. 2010. "Racial Earnings Inequlity in South Africa: An Assessment of Policy Options," *Journal of Policy Modelling* 32(6): 703–718.

Robertson, Raymond. 2004. "Relative Prices and Wage Inequality: Evidence from Mexico," *Journal of International Economics* 64(2): 387–409.

Rospabe, Sandrine. 2002. "How Did Labour Market Racial Discrimination Evolve After the End of Apartheid? An Analysis of the Evolution of Employment,

Occupational and Wage Discrimination in South Africa Between 1993 and 1999," *The South African Journal of Economics* 70(1): 185–217.

Sjoholm, Fredrik, and Robert E. Lipsey. 2006. "Foreign Firms and Indonesian Manufacturing Wages: An Analysis with Panel Data," *Economic Development and Cultural Change* 55(1): 102–221.

South African Reserve Bank. 2000–2008. *South African Reserve Bank Quarterly Bulletin*. Pretoria (September issues).

Statistics South Africa. 1995–1999. *October Household Surveys (OHS)*. Pretoria, South Africa: Statistics South Africa (producer); Pretoria: South African Data Archive (distributor).

UNCTAD (United Nations Conference on Trade and Development). 2009. *World Investment Report, International Bank for Development and Research. 2010*. New York.

Van Der Berg, Servaas et al. 2007. "Post-apartheid South Africa: Poverty and Distribution Trends in an Era of Globalization," World Institute for Development Economic Research (UNU-WIDER): Research Paper 2007/57.

Waldkirch, Andreas. 2010. "The Effects of Foreign Direct Investment in Mexico since NAFTA," *The World Economy* 33(5): 710–745.

Shirley Johnson-Lans is Professor of Economics at Vassar College. Her principal areas of teaching and research are Labor Economics, Health Care Economics, Gender Issues in Economics, and Income Inequality. Her publications include many journal articles and book chapters spanning a wide variety of subjects, from child marriage in rural India to an analysis of the Affordable Care Act. She is the author of the widely used textbook, *A Health Economics Primer* (Pearson: Addison-Wesley, 2006) which she is currently revising. She received her Ph.D. in Economics from Columbia University.

Patricia Jones is Project Manager and Researcher for the Urbanization in Developing Economies Project (Oxford University). Her current research focuses mainly on economic development in sub-Saharan Africa. She is particularly interested in the interplay between history, institutions, and long-run growth. Dr. Jones has held positions both within academia and in international organizations. She has publications in the *Economic Journal, Journal of Development Economics*, and *Journal of Comparative Economics*. She received her Ph.D. from Oxford University.

The Urban Wage Premium in Africa

Patricia Jones, Olivia D'Aoust and Louise Bernard

Abstract This chapter examines the size and sources of the urban wage premium in three African countries—Nigeria, Tanzania, and Uganda—using panel data on workers for the period 2009–2013. We ask three basic questions. First, is there any evidence that an urban wage premium exists in Africa? Second, what role, if any, does spatial sorting play in explaining this wage premium? And third, which demographic groups benefit the most from agglomeration effects? Our findings present new evidence on the role of cities in Africa. Specifically, we find strong evidence that an urban wage premium exists and is not explained solely by the spatial sorting of more skilled workers into African cities. However, there is considerable heterogeneity in who benefits from agglomeration effects. We find evidence that the urban wage premium is largest for workers in

This chapter is a part of a Global Research Program on Spatial Development of Cities, funded by the Multi Donor Trust Fund on Sustainable Urbanization of the World Bank and supported by the UK Department for International Development.

P. Jones (✉) · L. Bernard
Oxford University, Oxford, UK

O. D'Aoust
World Bank, Washington D.C., USA

S. Johnson-Lans (ed.), *Wage Inequality in Africa*, Global Perspectives on Wealth and Distribution, DOI 10.1007/978-3-319-51565-6_3

the primate city of each country and, in some cases, non-existent for workers in secondary cities. In addition, the urban wage premium is only found to be significant for male workers in all three countries studied.

Keywords Urban wage premium · Spatial sorting · Agglomeration effects

1 Introduction

Africa is urbanizing fast. Currently, 4.72 million people live in African cities and this number is expected to double in the next 25 years (UN, Nations 2015). By 2040 more than half of all Africans will be living in urban areas. How will this urbanization process affect the average African worker? If being employed in African cities cause worker productivity to rise, average wages should rise as the urban share of the population increases.[1] There is ample evidence from the rest of the world that cities generate many benefits (called agglomeration economies) which raise productivity (see reviews by Rosenthal and Strange 2004; Combes and Gobillon 2015).[2] Many of these benefits increase with scale: bigger cities generate larger productive advantages than smaller towns and rural areas. International evidence reveals that the elasticity of income with respect to city population is between 2% and 10% (Duranton 2015).

How do cities do this? Several channels are highlighted in the urban economics literature (see Duranton and Puga 2004 for a survey). First, cities facilitate the sharing of resources between workers and firms. Large markets in cities attract firms—including intermediate suppliers—which can reduce the price of a firm's inputs (resulting from tougher competition) and increase the range of inputs supplied. Shared labor markets make it easier for firms to hire new workers without having to spend a lot of time and money searching for the "right" applicant. In addition, cities facilitate the provision of certain goods or facilities (e.g., airports) which have to be supplied at large scale in order to be economically viable. And, finally, education is an important ingredient in generating knowledge spillovers because cities make it easier for workers to share information and learn from each other. Each of these mechanisms assumes that cities *make* workers and firms more productive. In other words, there is a causal relationship between increased economic density and increased productivity.

While numerous studies have examined the size and sources of the urban wage premium in advanced countries, much less is known about productive benefits of cities in developing countries. To date, the limited evidence that we have comes from only a handful of studies which use worker data from Colombia (Duranton 2016), India (Hnatkovska and Lahiri 2014) and Brazil (Cruz and Naticchioni 2012).[3] This is somewhat surprising, given that nearly all of the world's fastest growing cities—including many megacities—are located in the developing world. To partially fill this gap, we estimate the urban wage premium for three African countries: Nigeria, Tanzania, and Uganda. Similar to other studies, we find strong evidence that urban workers earn higher wages than equivalent workers in rural areas. Our estimates of the urban wage premium in Africa range from between 0.235 (log points) and 0.479 (log points), depending upon the country. These estimates are well within the range estimated for workers in more advanced economies, suggesting that African cities are generating similar agglomeration effects to cities elsewhere.[4]

But, is this the whole story? Much has been written about the different urbanization path taken by African countries (Gollin et al. 2016; Jedwab and Osei 2013; Fay and Opal 2000). Recent research suggests that African cities differ in four fundamental ways from cities in other developing regions. First, African countries are growing rapidly without a simultaneous increase in manufacturing activity (Fig. A.1). Second, African countries have a much smaller proportion of workers engaged in tradable production than cities elsewhere (Lall et al. 2017). Third, African cities are expensive places to live. Urban households pay about 77% more for housing and 26% more for food than households in other cities at comparable levels of economic development (Nakamura et al. 2016). And, finally, firms in African cities pay higher wages (at nominal exchange rates) than firms in other cities at comparable levels of economic development (Jones 2016). See Fig. A.2.

The finding that output prices and wages are higher in African cities than elsewhere is a major concern for it raises the possibility that Africa's high urban wages may not reflect "true" productivity differentials. Instead, it is possible that inefficient firms in the non-tradable sector are able to pass on their higher urban costs to consumers in the form of increased prices. In addition, inefficient firms in the tradable sector—where prices are fixed by international markets—may be unable to compete globally. While we cannot address this question directly,[5] we can take a first step toward identifying whether there is any empirical evidence to support a causal relationship between African cities and higher worker productivity. We do this by first examining the importance of spatial sorting in determining the urban wage premium, and then identifying how agglomeration benefits are spread across both cities and workers.

Much has been written on the extent to which more productive workers self-select into cities based on unobserved factors. High-ability workers may be attracted to cities because they have a greater preference for public amenities—like schools and cultural attractions—or because there is a greater demand for their skills by urban firms. To date, evidence on the existence of spatial sorting is mixed but some studies (Combes et al. 2008; Glaeser and Maré 2001) suggest it plays a prominent role in explaining the observed urban wage premium in advanced economies. From a policy perspective, it is important to identify whether cities raise worker productivity (cities generate agglomeration effects) or simply attract more productive workers (cities result from spatial sorting). If agglomeration effects are important, understanding the different sources of these effects (e.g., sharing, matching, and learning) and their relative magnitudes is important. Likewise, if spatial sorting is important, understanding why high-skilled workers prefer to live in cities rather than rural areas is a key policy question. The answers to these questions lie at the very heart of why cities exist and their role in the development process.

In this study, we address these questions by presenting new evidence on the productivity-enhancing role of African cities. We proceed in several steps. First, we estimate the urban wage premium using standard OLS pooled regressions. This is an appropriate model as long as our specification includes all individual characteristics that affect both sorting and wages. If there are missing variables, the OLS estimates will be biased. Next, we consider estimating the urban wage premium using a fixed effects (FE) model. This model controls for all unobserved, individual worker characteristics that do not vary over time. A well-known weakness of this approach, however, is that identification is based solely on migrants who may not be representative of the average, urban worker. Unfortunately, this is the case for all three of our samples which, given the short time period covered by the panels, include only a small number of migrants. As a result, we are skeptical that the FE results would generate unbiased estimates of the urban wage premium.[6]

Therefore, our next step is to re-estimate the wage equation using real wages (rather than nominal wages) as the dependent variable. As pointed out by Glaeser and Maré (2001, 321): "If real wages are not higher in large cities, then ability levels are not higher in those cities as well." And, finally, we estimate the potential importance of unobservable skills in generating the urban wage premium using the same method proposed by Murphy and Topel (1990). Specifically, we presume that workers' unobservable skills have about the same effect on wage determination as workers' observable skills. We then estimate the impact of workers' observable skills and "net out" their effects from our wage estimates.

As a preview of our results, we find little evidence that spatial sorting plays a major role in determining the urban wage premium in Africa. This suggests that African cities are generating significant agglomeration effects (assuming that the estimated wage differentials reflect "true" productivity differentials). However, our results are not entirely optimistic. Our data indicate that agglomeration benefits are not evenly spread across urban workers. In fact, once we control for the type of city where an individual works, we find no evidence of an urban wage premium outside of the primate city in either Nigeria or Tanzania. This suggests that secondary cities in both Nigeria and Tanzania are not generating significant agglomeration effects. Furthermore, we find that male workers employed in the primate city earn significantly higher wages than their rural counterparts but female workers do not. Finally, we find mixed evidence of a complementarity between skills and economic density across our three countries.

2 Why Do We Care About the Urban Wage Premium?

The urban wage premium provides one measure of the productive benefits of cities. When markets are competitive, average wages reflect the average marginal product of labor so higher urban wages (all else equal) indicate that workers employed in cities earn more than they would if they were employed in rural areas. Econometrically, problems arise with the "all else equal" condition. It is hard to control for all individual characteristics (e.g., quality of education, ambition) correlated with productivity. The econometric problems associated with estimating the "true" urban wage premium have led to two different hypotheses as to why a positive, urban wage gap is found in so many data sets.

The first assumes that cities generate productive advantages which raise the productivity of workers. That is, cities (because they have increased economic density) *cause* workers to be more productive:

2.1 Cities → Higher Productivity

International evidence provides strong support for this view: there is ample evidence that an urban wage premium exists in most cities in the developed world and that the size of this wage premium rises as cities get larger (see Duranton 2008 for a review). For instance, workers who live in the 30 largest metropolitan areas in the United States earn 33% more than workers who live outside these areas (Glaeser and Maré 2001). Similar estimates have been found for urban workers in other countries.

While few economists would dispute the claim that urban workers earn higher nominal wages than rural workers, there is less agreement on why such a wage premium exists. Some economists argue that cities do not raise productivity. Instead, they simply attract more productive workers who may have a greater preference for city amenities—like cultural attractions and universities—or who may be attracted to cities because there is greater demand for their skills. If this hypothesis is correct, the causality between productivity and city size is reversed. That is, cities grow because they attract more productive workers.

2.2 Higher Productivity → Larger Cities

Identifying the "true" underlying relationship between city size and productivity is important for designing appropriate urban policies. If cities raise worker productivity, it is important to identify what mechanisms (e.g., industrial clustering, knowledge spillovers, access to public infrastructure) have the largest productivity-enhancing effects. If cities simply attract more productive workers, it is important to identify why so many people wish to leave rural areas. However, distinguishing between the two hypotheses is not an easy task.

First, it is difficult for economists to control for all worker characteristics which may be correlated with productivity. Some characteristics—like ambition or innate ability—remain unobservable. Second, wage gaps are not identical to productivity gaps. Wages are only an indirect measure of worker productivity. While economic theory tells us that wages and productivity should be closely related, this relationship can break down in many settings like when labor and product markets are not perfectly competitive. Firms with market power may appear to have higher productivity than they actually do because they charge higher prices. Despite these caveats, the urban wage premium remains a useful measure of the productive advantage of cities. If an urban wage premium exists (even in nominal terms), it suggests that cities are generating some productive advantage to firms. Otherwise, firms (at least those in the tradable sector) would relocate to places where wages (and rents) were cheaper. The very fact that urban firms choose to remain in high-cost locations suggests that cities are productive places in which to operate a business.

3 Data and Estimation Strategy

Three panel data sets are employed to undertake a first estimation of the urban wage premium for African workers. We use the Nigeria National Household Survey (2010 and 2012), the Tanzania Panel Household Survey (2010–2011 and 2012–2013), and the Uganda National Panel Survey (2009, 2010, 2011, and 2012). Importantly, all three data sets include very precise geographic coordinates so it is possible to identify whether a worker lives in a large city, small city, or rural area.

To conduct our analysis, we first estimate the urban wage premium using a standard, pooled OLS regression:

$$w_{it} = \boldsymbol{x}'_{it}\beta + d_{it}\gamma + \lambda_t + \varepsilon_{it} \tag{1}$$

where w_{it} is the wage of worker at time t, d_{it} is a dummy variable which takes the value of 1 if the worker is employed in an urban area at time t, λ_t are time fixed effects, $\boldsymbol{x}'_{it}$ is a vector of worker and job characteristics, and ε_{it} is the error term. Equation (1) correctly identifies the urban wage premium only if we have data on all worker characteristics that affect both sorting and wages. If not, the urban wage premium will be biased. One method of addressing this problem is by including worker fixed effects in a panel specification (see Combes et al. 2008; De la Rocha and Puga 2015). That is, we could estimate the following FE regression:

$$w_{it} = \mu_i + \boldsymbol{x}'_{it}\beta + d_{it}\gamma + \lambda_t + \varepsilon_{it} \tag{2}$$

where μ_i is the worker fixed effect. A well-known weakness of this model, however, is that identification comes from migrants who may not be representative of the entire population.

De la Rocha and Puga (2015) argue that there is an additional source of worker heterogeneity that arises from the differential learning effects of cities. They argue that bigger cities generate larger learning effects than smaller cities. As a result, estimates of the urban wage premium will be biased if the wage equation does not include controls for workers' job histories (i.e., how much time they have spent working in large versus small cities). Unfortunately, we cannot control for the job histories of workers in our sample. However, our analysis suggests that few workers move from one sized city to another, at least during the period covered by our panel data.

4 Estimation Results

We begin our analysis by estimating Equation (1) using nominal wages. We restrict our sample to adults (aged 16–65) who work full time (20+ hours per week). Each regression controls for basic human capital variables—that is, age and its square, education, marital status, and gender—as well as a dummy variable for urban residence (*urban*), the logarithm of hours worked per week, and year fixed effects. The dependent variable is the logarithm of weekly earnings.

Several variations of this regression are estimated. To control for productivity differences among workers who are employed in different sectors and professions, we include industry and occupation fixed effects. In addition, we include a dummy variable indicating whether the worker is employed in the country's primate city—that is, Dar es Salaam[7] (for Tanzania), Kampala (for Uganda), and Lagos (for Nigeria). We include this control because we want to identify whether workers outside of the primate city are benefiting from economic density as well.

Let's examine the results for all workers (Table A.1). In Tanzania, the estimated urban wage premium is 32%[8] when only human capital controls are included in the wage equation (column 1). This estimate falls by more than half to 15% when we introduce industry and occupation FEs and include a control for Dar es Salaam (column 2). Notice that only the *Dar* dummy is significant in this specification, indicating that workers in secondary cities are not being paid higher nominal wages relative to their rural counterparts. By contrast, the estimated urban wage premium in Dar es Salaam is relatively large at 21%.

We find somewhat larger effects for urban workers in Uganda. The estimated wage premium in Uganda is over 60% when we control for human capital alone (column 3) and remains at 50% when the full model is estimated (column 4). More importantly, the *urban* dummy remains significant, even after we include a control for Kampala, indicating that workers in secondary cities also earn a wage premium. We do not find this result for the other two countries. However, the size of the estimated wage premium in the primate city is nearly the same across all three samples: 20% for Lagos (column 6), 21% for Kampala (column 4), and 22% for Dar es Salaam (column 2). If these wage differentials represent "true" productivity differentials, our results suggest that agglomeration effects in Africa's primate cities are about the same size as those estimated for cities elsewhere.[9] For comparison, Table A.2 lists the urban wage premia (relative to rural areas) which has been estimated for workers in other countries. These estimates range from 9% in the UK to 60% in France.

Our next step is to investigate the role of spatial sorting in explaining the observed urban wage premium. We use two estimation strategies. First, we re-estimate Equation (1) using real wages. As pointed out by Glaeser and Maré (2001), real wages should be significantly higher in cities when spatial sorting plays an important role in wage determination (Table A.3). And finally, we employ the same approach as that used by Murphy and Topel (1990) and Glaeser and Maré (2001) for estimating the potential effects of unobservable skills on the estimated (nominal) wage premium.

We find no evidence of spatial sorting in either Tanzania or Uganda when we re-estimate the wage equations using real wages (Table A.3).[10] While the urban wage premium is significant when we include only human capital controls, it loses significance once we introduce industry and occupation fixed effects. Unfortunately, we are unable to carry out this analysis for Nigeria due to a lack of price data. Corroborating evidence is also found when we "net out" the effects of workers' unobservable skills from the wage estimates. To derive these results, we presume that the importance of unobservable skills in explaining the wage differentials is similar to that of observable skills (Murphy and Topel 1990; Glaeser and Maré 2001). In all three countries, the gap in years of schooling between urban and rural workers is small: only 1.1 years for Nigeria; 1.5 years for Tanzania; and 1.2 years for Uganda. Furthermore, the estimated return to 1 year of education is 4.2% for Nigeria, 7.4% for Tanzania, and 7.8% for Uganda. By combing these two statistics, we estimate that the (potential) impact of unobservable skills accounts for approximately 5% of the urban wage premium in Nigeria, 11% in Tanzania, and 9% in Uganda.[11] When we control for these effects, the estimated wage (nominal) premium is still relatively large: 11% for workers in Dar es Salaam, 13% for workers in Kampala, and 16% for workers in Lagos. Both sets of results indicate that spatial sorting is not playing a large role in determining the urban (nominal) wage premium in Africa. In other words, the results suggest that significant agglomeration effects are being generated in each country, at least in the primate city.

The next question is: who benefits from these agglomeration effects? To address this question, we estimate Equation (1) for different samples of workers. Specifically, we estimate separate wage equations by gender and education level. The results from these regressions are reported in Tables A.4 and A.5. We find strong evidence that the benefits of agglomeration are not being spread evenly across all workers. Instead, male workers employed in the primate city benefit disproportionately from urbanization (Table A.4). That is, we find no evidence of an urban wage premium for female workers in any of the countries. Interestingly, we find mixed results with respect to a complementarity between skills and economic density. All forms of education are rewarded (in the form of higher wages) in Dar es Salaam but not in Tanzania's secondary cities. By contrast, only the less educated earn a wage premium in Uganda while the data indicate that there is no complementarity between skills and economic density in Nigeria. These results stand in stark contrast to what is usually found in more advanced economies. There is a great deal of empirical evidence that the benefits of agglomeration increase with skill level (Combes et al. 2012; De La Rocha and Puga 2015). However, Duranton (2016) finds no evidence of a complementarity between city size and skills for workers in Colombia.

5 Conclusion

Well-managed cities can bring large benefits to firms and workers. In this chapter, we examine the productive benefits of cities in Tanzania, Nigeria, and Uganda by investigating whether there is any evidence of an urban wage premium in each country. Our results indicate that most cities in Africa are not generating the same benefits to wage employees as cities in other countries. In both Tanzania and Nigeria, only workers in the primate city earn higher wages relative to their rural counterparts. By contrast, the data support the existence of an urban wage premium for all urban workers in Uganda.

From a policy point of view, it is important to identify whether these wage differentials reflect "true" productivity differentials. Economic theory predicts that workers are paid the value of their marginal product ($p \times$ MPL) when markets are perfectly competitive. It is possible that nominal wages in African cities are artificially high because inefficient firms pass on their higher costs to consumers in the form of increased prices. Indeed, recent research from the World Bank reveals that urban households in Africa pay about 77% more for housing and 26% more for food than urban households in other cities at comparable levels of economic development (Nakamura et al. 2016). Higher urban costs may be one reason why African firms have not been more successful at breaking into global markets (Venables 2016). While we cannot address this issue directly, we do investigate whether the urban wage premium is being driven by the spatial sorting of workers into cities—the first step toward identifying whether there is any causal relationship between increased economic density and increased worker productivity. The bulk of our empirical evidence indicates that spatial sorting does not play a large role in wage determination, suggesting that Africa's cities—at least its primate cities—are generating significant agglomeration effects.

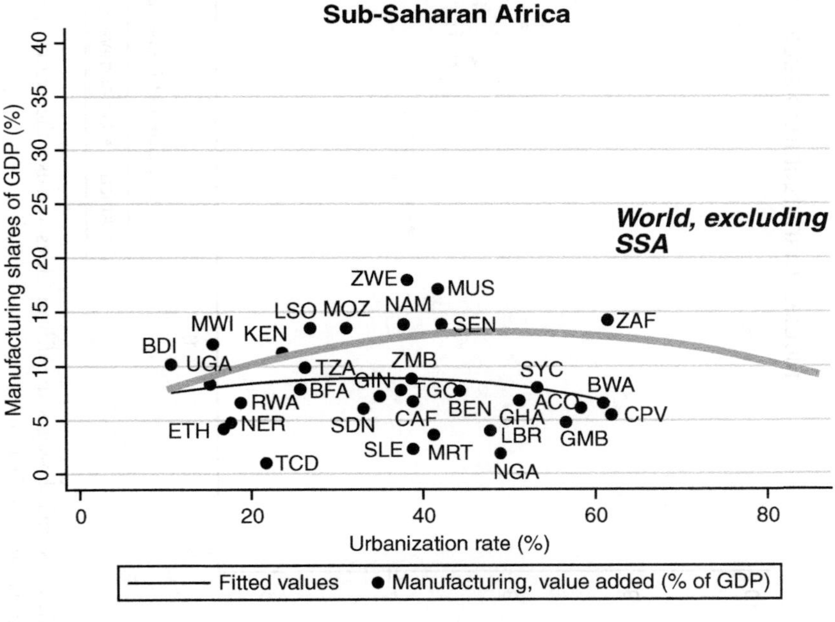

Fig. A.1 Urbanization and economic development. (*Source*: Authors' calculations based on World Bank Economic Surveys, 2015)

Fig. A.2 Nominal wages in African cities versus other cities. (*Source*: Authors' calculations based on World Bank Enterprise Surveys, 2015)

Table A.1 OLS estimates of the urban wage premium

	Tanzania (1)	*Tanzania* (2)	*Uganda* (3)	*Uganda* (4)	*Nigeria* (5)	*Nigeria* (6)
Urban	0.281**	0.144	0.479**	0.126*	0.184*	0.078
	(0.05)	(0.08)	(0.06)	(0.06)	(0.08)	(0.08)
Primate city	—	0.196**	—	0.188**	—	0.182*
		(0.06)		(0.06)		(0.09)
Primary	0.328**	0.153*	0.558**	0.175*	0.021	0.026
	(0.06)	(0.06)	(0.07)	(0.07)	(0.09)	(0.10)
Secondary	1.165**	0.613**	0.729**	0.124	0.394**	0.320**
	(0.07)	(0.09)	(0.204)	(0.20)	(0.11)	(0.11)
Higher	2.384**	1.637**	1.565**	0.604*	0.675**	0.391**
	(0.11)	(0.15)	(0.30)	(0.27)	(0.11)	(0.14)
Year FE	Yes	Yes	Yes	Yes	Yes	Yes
Industry	No	Yes	No	Yes	No	Yes
Occupation	No	Yes	No	Yes	No	Yes
Worker	No	No	No	No	No	No
Observations	3,693	2,830	2,929	2,894	2,000	1,981
R^2	0.358	0.421	0.214	0.376	0.131	0.24

Notes: Robust standard errors in parentheses. Standard errors are clustered by enumeration area. Dependent variable is log-weekly wages. All regressions control for gender, age and its square, marital status, and log (hours worked per week). Primate city corresponds to Dar es Salaam for Tanzania sample, Kampala for Uganda sample, and Lagos for Nigeria sample.

** indicates significant at 1% level.

* indicates significant at 5% level.

Table A.2 The urban wage premium for selected countries and years

Country	*Year(s)*	*Rural-urban wage gap %*		*Urban comparison group*	*Data*	*Author(s) and date*
		Nominal	*Real*			
Spain	2004–2009	55	—	Primate city: Madrid	Continuous sample of employment histories	De la Rocha and Puga (2015)
UK	1988–2008	9	—	Cities with > 100,000 workers in 1999	Annual Survey of Hours & Earnings (ASHE) and New Earnings Survey (NES)	D'Costa and Overman (2014)
India	1983 1993–2004 1999–2000 2004–2005 2009–2010		51 39 41 30 27	Urban areas have (1) a minimum population of 5,000; (2) at least 75% of the male population working in non-agricultural activities; and (3) a density of population of at least 1,000 people per square mile	Employment & Unemployment Surveys of the National Sample Survey (NSS)	Hnatkovska and Lahiri (2014)
Brazil	2002 2009	—	17 15	Ten largest metropolitan areas	National Household Survey (PNAD) for Brazil	Cruz and Naticchioni (2012)
France	1976–1996 (4-year intervals)	60	—	Primate city: Paris	Annual Social Data Declarations database for France	Combes et al. (2008)
United States	1980s and 1990s	23–32	—	Metropolitan areas with population > 1 million	Several used: 1990 Census, NLSY, CPS	Glaeser and Maré (2001)

Source: Compiled by Authors.

Table A.3 OLS estimates of the (real) urban wage premium

	Tanzania (1)	*Tanzania (2)*	*Uganda (3)*	*Uganda (4)*
Urban	0.155**	0.088	0.236**	−0.062
	(0.05)	(0.07)	(0.06)	(0.06)
Primate city	—	0.093	—	0.044
		(0.06)		(0.07)
Year FE	Yes	Yes	Yes	Yes
Industry	No	No	No	No
Occupation	No	No	No	No
Worker	No	No	No	No
Observations	3,593	2,734	2,908	2,894
R^2	0.328	0.40	0.16	0.33

Notes: Robust standard errors in parentheses. Dependent variable is log-weekly wages All regressions control for log (hours worked per week). Primate city corresponds to Dar es Salaam for Tanzania sample, Kampala for Uganda sample, and Lagos for Nigeria sample. Number of observations are slightly lower than that for wage equations using nominal wages due to missing price data for some workers.
** indicates significant at 1% level.

Table A.4 OLS estimates of the urban wage premium by gender

	Tanzania males (1)	*Tanzania females* (2)	*Uganda males* (3)	*Uganda females* (4)	*Nigeria males* (5)	*Nigeria females* (6)
Urban	0.160	0.059	0.115	0.143	0.103	0.219
	(0.09)	(0.12)	(0.06)	(0.09)	(0.10)	(0.19)
Primate city	0.257**	0.104	0.208*	0.192	0.284*	−0.051
	(0.07)	(0.10)	(0.08)	(0.10)	(0.12)	(0.12)
Year FE	Yes	Yes	Yes	Yes	Yes	Yes
Industry	Yes	Yes	Yes	Yes	Yes	Yes
Occupation	Yes	Yes	Yes	Yes	Yes	Yes
Worker	No	No	No	No	No	No
Observations	1,916	914	1,825	1,069	1,211	770
R^2	0.401	0.460	0.348	0.345	0.248	0.297

Notes: Robust standard errors in parentheses. Standard errors are clustered by enumeration area. Dependent variable is log-weekly wages. All regressions control for gender, age and its square, marital status, and log (hours worked per week). Primate city corresponds to Dar es Salaam for Tanzania sample, Kampala for Uganda sample, and Lagos for Nigeria sample.

** indicates significant at 1% level.

* indicates significance at 5% level.

Table A.5 OLS estimates of the urban wage premium by level of education

	Tanzania more educated (1)	*Tanzania less educated (2)*	*Uganda more educated (3)*	*Uganda less educated (4)*	*Nigeria more educated (5)*	*Nigeria less educated (6)*
Urban	0.237	0.146	–0.160	0.144*	0.071	0.104
	(0.163)	(0.08)	(0.34)	(0.06)	(0.10)	(0.13)
Primate City	0.218*	0.184*	–0.357	0.223**	0.208	–0.082
	(0.10)	(0.07)	(0.45)	(0.07)	(0.17)	(0.14)
Year FE	Yes	Yes	Yes	Yes	Yes	Yes
Industry	Yes	Yes	Yes	Yes	Yes	Yes
Occupation	Yes	Yes	Yes	Yes	Yes	Yes
Worker	No	No	No	No	No	No
Observations	695	2,135	82	2,812	952	1,029
R^2	0.38	0.24	0.58	0.376	0.33	0.21

Notes: Robust standard errors in parentheses. Standard errors are clustered by enumeration area. Dependent variable is log-weekly wages. All regressions control for gender, age and its square, marital status, and log (hours worked per week). Primate city corresponds to Dar es Salaam for Tanzania sample, Kampala for Uganda sample, and Lagos for Nigeria sample.

** indicates significant at 1% level.

* indicates significance at 5% level.

Notes

1. Urbanization can have a positive effect on rural wages as well. There may be backward linkages which increase the demand for agricultural products (Cali and Menon 2009) and/or rural workers may end up with greater land per person.
2. More recent studies include De La Rocha and Puga (2015); D'Costa and Overman (2014); Mion and Naticchioni (2009); Combes et al. (2008); Di Addario and Patacchini (2008); and Yankow (2006).
3. There is an older, well-established literature which estimates the difference in per capita consumption and poverty rates between urban and rural areas. These studies find that urban areas have higher per capita consumption and a lower incidence of poverty than rural areas. Examples include Squire (1981) and *World Development Report* (2010).
4. For example, Glaeser and Maré (2001) estimate an urban wage premium of between 0.071 (log points) and 0.441 (log points) for US workers.
5. To answer this question requires data on the physical output of workers. When using wages (or revenue-based measures of firm productivity) to measure agglomeration effects, it is impossible to determine whether higher wages (or establishment-level TFP) reflect higher physical productivity or simply higher prices.
6. We did estimate the urban wage premium using a fixed effects estimator but found inconsistent results compared to the other estimation techniques we used to identify the importance of sorting in explaining the wage premium. We are happy to provide these results on request.
7. While Dar es Salaam is the primate city of Tanzania, it is not its political capital. In 1973 the government announced that it was moving the capital to Dodoma. However, the transfer of political administration has been incomplete. A large number of government departments remain in Dar es Salaam and, of course, it remains the business capital and largest city in the country.
8. The percentage wage gap is calculated as $e^{\gamma} - 1$.
9. There is evidence from Africa that, on average, workers are paid the value of their marginal product. See Jones (2001). This study, however, covers only a few industries within the manufacturing sector in Ghana.
10. Real wages are calculated as nominal wages deflated by the Fischer price index for food. To calculate the Fischer price indices, we used price data collected as part of the Living Standards Measurement Survey (LSMS) community surveys in both Tanzania and Uganda. We are grateful to the Uganda Bureau of Statistics (UBOS) for releasing the Uganda price data to us.
11. Glaeser and Maré (2001, p. 330) find somewhat smaller size effects for workers' unobserved skills. In the US labor market, the dense metropolitan area wage effect is 5.2% smaller when they control for these variables.

References

Cali, M., and C. Menon. 2009. "Does Urbanization Affect Rural Poverty? Evidence From Indian Districts." SERC Discussion Paper No. 14.

Combes, P.P., and L. Gobillon. 2015. "The Empirics of Agglomeration Effects," In G. Duranton, V. Henderson, and W. Strange (Eds.), *Handbook of Regional and Urban Economics*. Vol. 5A. North-Holland: Amsterdam.

Combes, P.P., G. Duranton, and L. Gobillon. 2008. "Spatial Wage Disparities: Sorting Matters!," *Journal of Urban Economics* 68: 723–742.

Combes, P.P., G. Duranton, L. Gobillon, D. Puga, and S. Roux. 2012. "The Productivity Advantages of Large Cities: Distinguishing Agglomeration from Firm Selection," *Econometrica* 80(6): 2543–2594.

Cruz, B., and P. Naticchioni. 2012. "Falling Urban Wage Premium and Inequality Trends from Brazil," *Investigaciones Regionales* 24: 91–113.

D'Costa, S., and H. Overman. 2014. "The Urban Wage Growth Premium: Sorting or Learning," *Urban Economics* 48: 168–179.

De La Rocha, J., and D. Puga. 2015. "Learning by Working in Big Cities," Discussion Paper 9243, Centre for Economic Policy Research, Revised August 2015.

Di Addario, S., and E. Patacchini. 2008. "Wages and the City: Evidence From Italy," *Labour Economics* 15: 1040–1061.

Duranton, G. 2008. "Viewpoint: From Cities to Productivity Growth in Developing Countries," *The Canadian Journal of Economics* 41(3): 689–736.

Duranton, G. 2015. "Growing Through Cities in Developing Countries," *World Bank Research Observer* 30(1): 39–73.

Duranton, G. 2016. "Agglomeration Effects in Colombia," *Journal of Regional Science* 56(2): 210–238.

Duranton, G., and D. Puga 2004. "Micro-foundations of Urban Agglomeration Economies," In V Henderson and F Thisse, (Eds..), *Handbook of Regional and Urban Economics.* Vol. 4. North-Holland: Amsterdam.

Fay and Opal. 2000. "Urbanization Without Growth: A Not So Uncommon Phenomenon," Policy Research Working Paper 2412, World Bank, Washington, DC.

Glaeser, E., and D. C. Maré. 2001. "Cities and Skills," *Journal of Labor Economics* 19: 316–342.

Gollin, D., R. Jedwab, and D. Vollrath. 2016. "Urbanization With and Without Industrialization," *Journal of Economic Growth* 21: 35–70.

Hnatkovska, V., and A. Lahiri. 2014. "Structural Transformation and the Rural-Urban Divide," processed, Wharton School.

Jedwab, R., and R.D. Osei. 2013. "Is Structural Transformation Different in Sub-Saharan Africa? New Historical Evidence From Ghana," unpublished paper, George Washington University.

Jones, P. 2001. "Are Educated Workers Really More Productive?" *Journal of Development Economics* 64: 57–79.

Jones, P. 2016. "Closed for Business, High Urban Costs," unpublished paper, Department of Economics, University of Oxford.

Lall, S., V. Henderson, and A. Venables. 2017. *Africa's Cities: Opening Doors to the World*. Washington, DC: World Bank.

Mion, G., and P. Naticchioni. 2009. "The Spatial Sorting and Matching of Firms," *Canadian Journal of Economics* 42: 28–55.

Murphy, K.V., and R.H. Topel. 1990. "Efficiency Wages Reconsidered: Theory and Evidence," In Y.Weis and G. Fishelson (Eds.), *Advances in the Theory and Measurement of Efficiency Wages*. New York: MacMillan.

Nakamura, S., R. Harati, S.V. Lall, Y.M. Dikhanov, N. Hamadeh, W.V. Oliver, M.O. Rissanen, and M. Yamanaka. 2016. *Is Living in African Cities Expensive?* Unpublished paper, World Bank, Washington, DC.

Rosenthal, S., and W. Strange. 2004. "Evidence on the Nature and Sources of Agglomeration Economies". ch. 49, pp. 2119–2171," In J. V. Henderson and J. F. Thisse, (Eds.), *Handbook of Regional and Urban Economics*, Vol. 4. Amsterdam: Elsevier.

Squire, L. 1981. *Employment Policy in Developing Countries*. Oxford, UK: Oxford University Press.

United Nations. 2015. Department of Economic and Social Affairs, Population Division. World Population Prospects: The 2015 Revision. New York: United Nations.

Venables, A. 2016. "Breaking Into Tradables: Urban Form and Urban Function in a Developing City," unpublished paper, Department of Economics, University of Oxford.

Yankow, J. 2006. "Why Do Cities Pay More? An Empirical Investigation of Some Competing Theories of the Urban Wage Premium," *Journal of Urban Economics* 60: 139–161.

World Bank. 2010. *World Development Report 2009*. Washington, DC: World Bank.

Patricia Jones is Project Manager and Researcher for the Urbanization in Developing Economies Project (Oxford University). Her current research focuses mainly on economic development in sub-Saharan Africa. She is particularly interested in the interplay between history, institutions, and long-run growth. Dr. Jones has held positions both within academia and in international organizations. She has publications in the *Economic Journal*, *Journal of Development Economics*, and *Journal of Comparative Economics*. She received her Ph.D. from Oxford University.

Olivia D'OAoust is an Urban Economist at the World Bank Group. She has recently been focusing on the drivers and impediments of African cities' productivity and livability. Her work cuts across issues of urbanization, conflict/fragility, and disasters. Recent publications include articles in the *Journal of African Economies* and *World Bank Economic Review*. She received her Ph.D. in Economics from the European Center for Advanced Research in Economics and Statistics, Brussels.

Louise Bernard is a Research Assistant in Economics for the Urbanisation in Sub-Saharan Africa Research Project at Oxford University. Her ongoing research is focused on transportation infrastructure and its role in development and includes the development of a general equilibrium model for the city of Kampala, Uganda. She is the author of a working paper: Transport in a congested city: A computable equilibrium model applied to Kampala City (2016).

Gender-Based Wage Differentials and Employment in Post-Apartheid South Africa, 1995–2004

Shirley Johnson-Lans

Abstract This chapter investigates the trends in gender differentials in wages and employment over the first post-apartheid decade in South Africa, a time when social policy was focused on race. Using merged household and worker data sets, a two-stage regression estimation strategy is used to construct gender-based wage differentials, controlling for industry, occupation, region, and demographic and human capital variables (years of education, experience, and experience squared). The resulting male/female log wage differentials are the dependent variables in the second-stage regressions. The effect of labor force characteristics (within-sector proportion unionized, proportion black, proportion female, average hours worked per week, and average years of experience), industrial sector, and globalization

The author gratefully acknowledges the helpful comments of Colleen Chrisinger, Patricia Jones, and Sarah Pearlman; the help of research assistants Joseph Coniglio and Maria Urquiza and Ford summer fellows, Sharon Freiman and Stephanie Owen. The research was supported by a Ford Foundation Summer Research Fellowship.

S. Johnson-Lans (✉)
Vassar College, Poughkeepsie, New York, USA

S. Johnson-Lans (ed.), *Wage Inequality in Africa*, Global Perspectives on Wealth and Distribution, DOI 10.1007/978-3-319-51565-6_4

(measured by foreign direct investment/capital stock in sector and year) on these wage differentials is investigated. The study finds some evidence of a decline in the gender wage gap over the period 1995–2004. And as is true in many other economies, women appear to do less well, for example, there is a wider gender gap in wages, in environments where workers have higher average levels of skill or experience. Regressions are also run on female/male employment ratios, using a similar set of control variables. Evidence is found, at least for white workers, that the proportion of women in the employed labor force increases over the decade. The effects of unionization and globalization on employment of women are also investigated.

Keywords Gender wage gap · Post-apartheid · Female/male employment ratios

1 Introduction

In the history of social and political movements, it has not been uncommon for movements promoting racial equality to ignore gender inequality. One need only look at the absence of enfranchisement of women in the post-Civil War period in the United States, when nineteenth-century feminists devoted considerable effort to promoting voting rights for African-American men, only to find their own enfranchisement delayed until 1920. The last minute addition of sex to the other protected categories (race, color, religion, and national origin) in the drafting of the legislation for Title VII of the Civil Rights Act of 1964 was widely believed to have only been accomplished because a member of the House of Representatives who hoped to see the civil rights legislation defeated thought including gender would lead to its downfall.[1]

The decade following the end of apartheid in South Africa is an interesting one to study in this regard. Although South African public policy toward labor was clearly aimed at eradicating racial discrimination, labor legislation, including that which promoted unionization, may have had adverse effects on women workers. Post-apartheid South Africa was opened up to more international trade and inflows of foreign direct investment (FDI), and this appears to have favored capital rather than labor-intensive production. Thus this period, although accompanied by a growth in real wages for those employed, was also associated with high rates of unemployment, and female unemployment rates far exceeded those of males.

This chapter examines patterns in gender-based wage differentials and gender differences in employment in South Africa over the period 1995–2004, for each of the three main racial groups, controlling for demographic and human capital variables, occupation, industrial sector, industry characteristics, degree of penetration of FDI in sector, and region. It thus focuses on what is often called the "residual" gender wage differential, aiming to illuminate the part of the wage differential that can be attributed solely to gender. This is often identified as discrimination, although it may also represent unobserved differences related to productivity (quality of schooling, attitudes toward work, etc.)

Several large data sets are employed. Merging the household and worker files of the October Household Surveys (OHS) for 1995–1999 and the Labour Force Surveys (LFS) for 2000–2004, gender wage differentials are estimated for each year and for each of five large industrial sectors in which women represent a substantial part of the labor force (agriculture, finance, manufacturing, services, and trade). Workers whose usual employment is 20 or more hours per week are included. Separate equations are estimated for each of the three main racial groups: white, black, and colored.[2] In Stage I of the analysis, fairly standard Mincer wage equations are estimated from individual data for each year, industrial sector, and race. The resulting coefficients (male/female log wage differentials) are then used as the dependent variables in the second-stage regressions.

Evidence of a decline in the gender wage gap over the decade 1995–2004 is found, but it is only statistically significant for colored workers. However, if one relaxes slightly the stringency of the significance requirement, there is an observed tendency toward a decline over the period in the magnitude of the gender wage gap for black and white workers as well.

The trend in proportion of female employees in these five industrial sectors is also investigated, taking account of degree of globalization and sector fixed effects as well as average worker characteristics within sector. When the full set of worker and industry covariates are included in the regression, positive statistically significant effects are found, but only for whites. However, when the proportion of employees who are female is regressed only on time (year) all three racial groups show gains in the proportion of women workers over the decade.

The remainder of this chapter is organized as follows: Section 2 provides some background information about the South African labor market.

Section 3 describes the data and empirical strategies used and presents the empirical results. Section 4 provides a discussion and some tentative conclusions.

2 The Post-Apartheid South African Labor Market

The most dramatic fact about the South African labor market in the post-apartheid decade is the very high and increasing unemployment rate. According to Rhys Jenkins, South Africa also experienced decreases in total employment in the formal labor market in both the periods 1990–1995 and 1996–2001, with a more marked decline (–1.6 percent) in the latter period. This trend was particularly pronounced in the manufacturing sector, where employment declined by 2.9 percent (Jenkins 2006, 650). The degree of globalization of the South African economy appears to have been a factor contributing to the state of the labor market during this period. Although economic liberalization was associated with economic growth, it was also associated with job shedding as business became more internationally competitive (Van Der Berg et al. 2007). An increase in trade was associated with a shift to more capital intensive sectors, and productivity increases led to a further reduction in unskilled jobs, particularly in manufacturing (Edwards 2004). An effect of globalization was therefore the retrenchment of workers, most notable in particular industries. For instance, a study of the South African textile industry found that opening the textile market to imports led to a pattern of "job-shedding output growth, particularly of unskilled jobs" (Bejuidenhout et al. 2007, 546). Import substitution exaggerated the situation, especially as the number of workers located in the export sector was a very small proportion of the employed labor force.

However, Rhys Jenkins notes that "although trade liberalization has been a factor reducing employment, those firms who have lost market share only account for a limited proportion of the total lay-offs that have occurred in South Africa" (Jenkins 2004, 8). He attributes the rest of the lay-off of workers to the sluggish growth of the South African economy in general. Although there was a surge of capital inflow into South Africa at the end of apartheid, it did not reach expected levels, and the outflow of FDI was greater than the inflow in some years (1995, 1996, 1998, 1999).

Moreover, a major part of the foreign investment into South Africa in the 1990s was in the form of mergers and acquisitions of local firms and those recently privatized (Jenkins 2006, 657–658). An analysis of the composition of capital flows into South Africa during this period also contributes to an understanding of why globalization may have had negative effects on South African workers (Ahmed et al. 2007; Funke et al. 2005). The capital inflows were largely in the form of portfolio inflows rather than investment used to augment productive capacity.[3]

According to Bhorat and Oosthuizen, an accurate characterization of the labor market in this period is that the South African labor force grew at a rate exceeding that which could be absorbed by the growth in the economy, despite large capital inflows (Bhorat and Oosthuizen 2005). Formal sector wages rose during the 1990s despite pressures from globalization, but since the wage elasticity of demand for labor also grew during this period, the negative effect of higher wages on employment increased over time (Jenkins 2006, 662–663). Since productivity grew more rapidly than wages, labor's share of gross output declined over the first post-apartheid decade (Wakeford 2004).

A working paper from the Development Policy Research Unit, University of Cape Town, provides detailed information on employment and labor force characteristics, 1995–2002, using two main data sources, the OHS and the LFS. The official unemployment rate (those actually seeking jobs) in South Africa rose from 17.6 to 30.5 percent between 1995 and 2002, while the broad unemployment rate rose from 30.8 to 40.8 percent (Bhorat and Oosthuizen 2005, Table 15, p. 33). The most rapidly growing demographic group in the labor force was African female first-time job seekers who were urban, under 35 years of age, and "possessing some level of secondary education" (Bhorat and Oosthuizen 2005, 6).

Wage inequality appears to have increased during the first post-apartheid decade in South Africa. Whether this is primarily related to globalization is, however, an open question. The effects of FDI on labor markets are complex. Figini and Gorg find that the effect of inward FDI on wage inequality varies by development level of a country. Wage inequality increases with FDI in developing countries but this effect diminishes with further increases in FDI and even reverses in direction in highly developed economies (Figini and Gorg 2011, 1473).

Domestic policy toward labor was also an important factor. Pro-labor policies of the African National Congress (ANC) government increased the power of labor unions, but by the end of the 1990s regulations and amendments to these laws tended to weaken the power of unions. The macroeconomic policy of the ANC government was not unambiguously labor friendly in that the GEAR (Growth, Employment, and Redistribution) policies from 1996 on aimed to improve the country's international competitiveness by "attracting foreign capital, cutting budget deficits and restraining wages"

(Jenkins 2006, 662). Thus GEAR may have tended to undermine the anti-discrimination legislation as well as limit the power of unions.

Moreover, there is no general agreement about the magnitude or even the direction of the effect of union power on the wage distribution in South Africa. An article by Bhorat et al. finds a much lower union wage premium for African workers than do many previous studies (Bhorat et al. 2012). And although the union wage premium in South Africa declined over time, Ntuli and Kwenda find that in recent years the net effect of unionization, at least for African males, appears to have been to increase racial wage inequality (Ntuli and Kwenda 2014). Casale and Posel, on the other hand, found that unions tended to compress the black/white male wage differential (Casale and Posel 2011).

2.1 *Studies of Gender Wage Differentials in South Africa*

Studies of gender-based wage differentials in South Africa have tended to be cross-sectional and to focus on a few of the immediate pre- and post-apartheid years. Timothy Hinks estimated gender wage differentials for each of the four main racial groups in 1995 (Hinks 2002). He found the gender differentials for whites to be greater than for colored or black workers, with Indian/Asian wage differentials lying somewhere in between. He attributed this to the fact that employment for black and colored males and females tend to be clustered at the low end of the wage scale and suggested that if education and labor market opportunities for black and colored workers improve, the gender wage gap may also widen. Serumaga-Zake and Naude analyzed wage differentials in 1995 for the Northwest province. Taking account of productivity differentials and a variety of individual characteristics, they found discrimination to be the source of about 50 percent of the gender wage gap (Serumaga-Zake and Naude 2001). Carola Grun studied gender discrimination in the two years immediately following the end of apartheid, taking into account the probability of finding employment as well as wage differentials. She found significant gender-based wage differentials for white women, but African and colored women faced more discrimination in hiring (Grun 2004). Daniela Casale, looking at cross-sectional data for several years during the period 1995–2001, found a "feminization" of the South African labor market in which women were predominantly mired in insecure low-paying jobs (Casale 2004). She found that only white women had been able to move into the small number of higher-level jobs open to women. Her examination of the South African labor market led her to the conclusion that there was little overall improvement in female wages, especially as women were pushed into the labor force in ever larger numbers out of economic necessity, with resulting high levels of female unemployment.

Several studies address the effect of unionization on the gender gap in wages. As with racial wage differentials, there is some disagreement about the effect of unions. Casale and Posel found that the gender wage gap tended to be larger in more highly unionized sectors of the South African economy (contrasting with their findings about the effect of unions on the racial wage gap). They found this to be the case even when controlling for occupational sorting by gender into union and non-union employment (Casale and Posel 2011). A study by Ntuli, based on 2001 and 2007 survey data, found a large gender wage gap among African workers in both union membership and unionized jobs (Ntuli 2012). Nonetheless, he argues that much of the gender gap in wages would be closed if women had the same access to the higher paying union jobs as do men. The implication of all of these studies taken together seems to be that women would benefit from receiving a union wage premium if they had better access to unionized jobs, but although their average wage might improve, given the larger gender gap in wages in unionized sectors of the economy, their position relative to males employed in the same (unionized) industries might not improve or even worsen.

This chapter will attempt to advance our knowledge about the gender wage gap and gender employment gap for white, black, and colored workers in South Africa, 1995–2004.

3 Data, Estimation Techniques, and Empirical Results

3.1 Data

This study employs two large nationally representative household surveys. For 1995–1999, the October Household Surveys (OHS) are used.[4] For 2000–2004, the ILO's Labor Force Surveys (LFS) replaced the OHS. Both surveys collected data on workers 15 years of age and older. Population weights were applied to adjust for variations from year to year in proportions of racial groups and of men and women in the samples. Data for 1995 through 2000 are independent cross-sectional samples. The LFS is, however, a rotating panel. Beginning in 2001, 20 percent of the households were replaced every six months. Because of this rapid rotation, we do not expect any serious distortion in the estimations using these data.

Merged worker and household surveys for both the OHS and LFS contain a wealth of information about individual workers including wages, hours worked, work history (e.g., number of years in labor force) industry, occupation, region, and personal characteristics such as race, gender, marital status, and years of education. In the OHS, wage data are absolute values for about 70 percent of the samples. For workers who answered only with respect to income category, the logarithmic mean of the two endpoints of the wage range was used. For years in which the LFS was used, wages are computed as (usual) weekly income divided by average hours worked per week. The samples used in this paper include workers 15–65 years of age employed for 20 hours or more in a typical week.

The analysis by sector includes the industrial sectors: agriculture, finance, manufacturing, services (excluding personal services), and trade. Several sectors were excluded because they employed too few women (mining, construction, transportation) or because the numbers of workers in the sample was too small (utilities). Workers employed by exterior organizations and foreign governments are excluded. The resulting aggregate sample sizes are shown below.

Year	*1995 OHS*	*1996 OHS*	*1997 OHS*	*1998 OHS*	*1999 OHS*	*2000 LFS*	*2001 LFS*	*2002 LFS*	*2003 LFS*	*2004 LFS*
n	23,172	40,253	24,518	46,643	63,107	61,900	63,553	49,236	60,147	66,169

The occupational categories for which dummy variables are constructed (and used in the Stage I regressions) are manager, professional, technical, sales, skilled agricultural worker, artisan, operator, and unskilled laborer, with unskilled laborer treated as the omitted category. Education is measured by number of years of schooling, and experience is measured by number of years beyond age 14 in which the person was in the labor force. Marital status is indicated by a dummy variable, "married," which is defined as married, spouse present, in the current year.

Information on FDI and capital stock in industrial sector was obtained from *the Quarterly Bulletin of Statistics* which publishes data collected by the South African Reserve Bank. The variable "FDI/k" used in this study is defined as the ratio of the stock of foreign direct investment to gross capital stock in each major industrial sector (defined at the two-digit level). FDI and gross capital stock are measured in millions of rand deflated to year 2000 values. Both FDI and size of capital stock vary by year and sector, permitting the inclusion of year and industry fixed effects in the regression analysis.

3.2 *Estimation Procedure: Wage Differentials*

A two-stage estimation process is employed. Stage I regressions estimate separate wage equations for workers of each racial group in each of the five two-digit industry sectors described above for each of the 10 years. The log wage equations make use of the individual household and worker data and control for a set of personal characteristics (gender, marital status, education,[5] years of experience, years of experience squared, occupation, union status, and region). The wage equation is specified as

$$LogW_i = \alpha + X_i\beta + Z_j\gamma + \varepsilon_{ij}$$

where

W_i is the weekly wage of worker i,

X_i is a vector of personal characteristics, occupation, and union status of worker i,

Z_j is a vector of mutually exclusive dummy variables for region,

ε_{ij} is the random disturbance term, α is the intercept term, and β and γ are the parameter vectors.

The coefficient for the variable "female" is the contribution of gender to the log wage and thus can be interpreted as the gender component of the wage differential. The (negative) signs of the coefficient are reversed and the coefficients converted to percentage wage differentials. These resulting male/female percentage wage differentials are shown in Table 1. They are the left-hand dependent variables in the second stage regression analysis.

The Stage II wage equation is specified as

$$D_{ij} = \alpha + X_{ij}\beta + Y_j\gamma + Z\lambda + \varepsilon_{ij},$$

where

D_{ij} is the male/female percentage wage differential in year i and sector j,

X_{ij} is a vector of average sector characteristics (percentage unionized, percentage black, percentage female, average hours per week, average years of experience, FDI/k) in year and sector,

Table 1. Stage I regression coefficients: gender effect on log-wage differentials

	Year and race	*Agriculture*	*Manufacturing*	*Trade*	*Services*	*Finance*
1995	White	0.794**	0.443**	0.468**	0.459**	0.292**
		(0.1866)	(0.0710)	(0.0635)	(0.0318)	(0.0629)
	Black	0.238**	0.318**	0.192**	0.159**	0.088[a]
		(0.0330)	(0.0323)	(0.0318)	(0.0238)	(0.0797)
	Colored	0.294**	0.180**	0.304**	0.267**	0.124
		(0.0384)	(0.0444)	(0.0489)	(0.0448)	(0.0732)
1996	White	0.624[a]	0.369**	0.346**	0.218**	0.493**
		(0.4993)	(0.1194)	(0.1186)	(0.0591))	(0.1008)
	Black	0.209**	0.394**	0.359**	0.159**	0.131
		(0.0715)	(0.0523)	(0.0537)	(0.0356)	(0.0733)
	Colored	0.345**	0.469**	0.264*	0.309**	0.120
		(0.0913)	(0.0730)	(0.1032)	(0.0631)	(0.1464)
1997	White	0.294[a]	0.276**	0.436**	0.305**	0.404**
		(0.3336)	(0.0898)	(0.0864)	(0.0583)	(0.0895)
	Black	0.261**	0.400**	0.252**	0.352**	0.222**
		(0.0440)	(0.0323)	(0.0343)	(0.0140)	(0.0681)
	Colored	0.264**	0.209**	0.270**	0.499**	0.309**
		(0.0517)	(0.0438)	(0.0583)	(0.0430)	(0.1068)
1998	White	1.289**	0.424**	0.476**	0.418**	0.040[a]
		(0.3919)	(0.0960)	(0.1168)	(0.0685)	(0.1357)
	Black	0.102*	0.488**	0.261**	0.381**	0.025[a]
		(0.0490)	(0.0560)	(0.0472)	(0.0343)	(0.0986)
	Colored	0.308**	0.245**	0.290**	0.355**	0.342*
		(0.0664)	(0.0657)	(0.0749)	(0.0757)	(0.1335)
1999	White	0.312	0.430**	0.384**	0.351**	0.412**
		(0.2047)	(0.1149)	(0.0940)	(0.0293)	(0.0828)
	Black	0.173**	0.495**	0.339**	0.311**	0.338**
		(0.0297)	(0.0377)	(0.0377)	(0.0320)	(0.0567)
	Colored	0.244**	0.400**	0.379**	0.518**	0.270**
		(0.0380)	(0.0714)	(0.0695)	(0.0756)	(0.0864)
2000	White	1.650*	0.315[a]	1.211**	0.321	0.129[a]
		(0.7321)	(0.4850)	(0.3618)	(0.2594)	(0.3223)
	Black	0.109	0.621**	0.301**	0.426**	0.375**
		(0.0684)	(0.0820)	(0.0764))	(0.0797)	(0.1233)
	Colored	0.217**	0.602**	0.516*	0.723**	0.066[a]
		(0.0636)	(0.1491)	(0.2115)	(0.2118)	(0.3607)
2001	White	1.033*	0..446**	0.379**	0.460**	0.531**
		(0.4863)	(0.1353)	(0.1032)	(0.0712)	(0.1287)
	Black	0.102**	0.480**	0.322**	0.324**	0.345**
		(0.0237)	(0.0288)	(0.0285)	(0.0271)	(0.0490)
	Colored	0.219**	0.477**	0.257**	0.424**	0.314*
		(0.0384)	(0.0591)	(0.0640)	(0.0632)	(0.1266)

(*continued*)

Table 1. (continued)

Year and race		*Agriculture*	*Manufacturing*	*Trade*	*Services*	*Finance*
2002	White	-.091[a]	0.143[a]	0.051[a]	0.204*	0.242
		(0.1966)	(0.1321)	(0.1182)	(0.1007)	(0.1475)
	Black	0.030[a]	0.210**	0.065*	0.121**	0.029[a]
		(0.0266)	(0.0323)	(0.0287)	(0.0294)	(0.0363))
	Colored	0.168**	0.115	0.134**	0.192**	0.037[a]
		(0.0340)	(0.0609)	(0.0643)	(0.0659)	(0.0778)
2003	White	0.634[a]	-0.118[a]	0.290**	0.384**	0.064[a]
		(0.5904)	(0.1139)	(0.1122)	(0.0954)	(0.1237)
	Black	0.118**	0.341**	0.164**	0.260**	0.096**
		(0.0206)	(0.0283)	(0.0250)	(0.0259)	(0.0337)
	Colored	0.228**	0.275**	0.225**	0.389**	0.212*
		(0.0304)	(0.0552)	(0.0604)	(0.0648)	(0.1017)
2004	White	0.234[a]	0.472*	0.249[a]	0.291*	0.540**
		(0.7291)	(0.2035)	(0.1788)	(0.1150)	(0.2065)
	Black	0.215**	0.398**	0.233**	0.323**	0.187**
		(0.0276)	(0.0349)	(0.0342)	(0.0322)	(0.0462)
	Colored	0.202**	0.172**	0.351**	0.380**	0.206**
		(0.0367)	(0.0658)	(0.0697)	(0.0608)	(0.0727)

* indicates significance at a 0.05 level.
** indicates significance at a 0.01 level.
[a]The value of coefficients that were not even marginally statistically significant, for example, those for which the *p* value was > 0.20 are entered as 0s in Stage II regressions. Few coefficients fall in this area. Most were significant or marginally significant or had *p* values > 0.6.

Υ_j is a vector of mutually exclusive dummy variables for industrial sector,
Z is a time trend variable,
ε_{ij} is random disturbance term,
α is the intercept term, and β, γ δ, and λ are the parameter vectors.

Several specifications of the model are estimated in order to give a clearer picture of how sector characteristics and sector fixed effects affect the wage differentials. Specification (1) includes only the components of X_{ij} excluding FDI/k, for example, the proportion of black workers, the proportion of female workers, the proportion of workers in unions, average hours per week, and average years of experience. Specification (2) adds (FDI/k). Specification (3) adds industrial sector fixed effects, Υ_j, with manufacturing the omitted category; and specification (4) adds a time trend variable, Z.

3.3 *Empirical Results: Gender Gap in Wages*

Tables 2a, 2b, and 2c show the Stage II regression results for white, black, and colored workers. For colored workers there is a significant decline over the period in the gender wage gap. It is found to decline by about 2.4 percent per year over the decade. For both black and white workers, there is also some indication that the wage gap may be declining over time. For whites, a downward trend in the wage differential of approximately 7.5 percent per annum (significant at a $p = 0.101$ level) is found. For blacks a more modest downward trend, 2.1 percent

Table 2a. Wage differentials: white

Independent variables	*(1)*	*(2)*	*(3)*	*(4)*
Year				−0.0754569[c]
				(0.0448465)
Prop_FDI		0.0413788	0.0451313	0.0451313
		(0.0936879)	(0.1043497)	(0.1043497)
Prop_union	−0.137407	−0.0388691	−0.3819768	0.1833879
	(0.3790773)	(0.3511143)	(0.5153082)	(0.741636)
Prop_female	0.2711452	0.1940545	−0.8346283	−0.7534776
	(0.483209)	(0.5010454)	(1.372661)	(1.320647)
Prop_black	−0.0674458	−0.2500675	−1.260134	−1.287295
	(0.3790773)	(0.4581573)	(0.8524284)	(1.633926)
Avg_hrs_wk	0.0143684	0.0061505	0.0319846	0.0277598
	(0.0292547)	(0.0368722)	(0.507101)	(0.0506866)
Avg_yrs_exp	0.0266547	−0.5583327	0.0632669[b]	0.065393*
	(0.030255)	(0.0656563)	(0.0355185)	(0.0355185)
Agri[a]			−0.3315823	−0.6266502
			(0.6549413)	(0.3982605)
Trade			0.1526786	−0.1766469
			(0.2556433)	(0.5407671))
Service			0.3486415	0.3159756
			(0.4477462)	(0.4402009)
Finance			−0.2871992	0.7979324
			(0.3238201)	(0.7566341)
No. of observations	50	50	50	50
R^2	0.0605	0.0695	0.1053	0.1919

* indicates significance at 0.05 level.
[a]Manufacturing is the omitted industrial category.
[b]Significant at $p = 0.083$ level.
[c]Significant at $p = 0.101$ level.

Table 2b. Wage differentials: black

Independent variables	*(1)*	*(2)*	*(3)*	*(4)*
Year				−0.0210365[c]
				(0.0117377)
Prop_FDI		−0.027394	0.0019299	0.0317692
		(0.0190483)	(0.0168538)	(0.0250335)
Prop_union	0.473965**	0.40873**	0.161871	0.3194879
	(0.1550205)	(0.152653)	(0.2264371)	(0.2303395)
Prop_female	−0.392415	−0.134379	0.2676222	0.290246
	(0.26246)	(0.3413785)	(0.5984807)	(0.5764829)
Prop_black	0.069726	0.190626	0.9000433	1.610236
	(0.1894371)	(0.1892996)	(0.8082154)	(1.11022)
Avg_hrs_wk	−0.000366	0.0050747	−0.0086135	−0.0097913
	(0.0097403)	(0.0107915)	(0.0166848)	(0.0173207)
Avg_yrs_exp	−0.005618	−0.0094047	0.0300915[b]	0.0306843[b]
	(0.0094655)	(0.0094211)	(0.0170935)	(0.0173877)
Agri[a]			−0.3702121*	−.4524735*
			(0.1727884)	(0.1928359)
Trade			−0.3214746*	−0.0585247
			(0.139537)	(0.1416128)
Service			−0.2421056	−0.251214
			(0.1679002)	(0.163596)
Finance			0.2227007	0.5252223
			(0.4149915)	(0.5360736)
No. of observations	50	50	50	50
R^2	0.1866	0.2043	0.3973	0.4273

* indicates significance at a 0.05 level.
** indicates significance at a 0.01 level.
[a]Manufacturing is the omitted industrial category.
[b]Significant at $p = 0.086$ level.
[c]Significant at $p = 0.081$ level.

Table 2c. Wage differentials: colored

Independent variables	*(1)*	*(2)*	*(3)*	*(4)*
Year				−0.0238703*
				(0.0117766)
Prop_FDI		−0.001478	−0.0121151	0.0217438
		(0.0141295)	(0.0133813)	(0.0230967)
Prop_union	0.19944	0.1959203	0.382038	0.5608874[b]
	(0.1613483)	(0.1674947)	(0.2925356)	(0.3020281)

(continued)

Table 2c. (continued)

Independent variables	*(1)*	*(2)*	*(3)*	*(4)*
Prop_female	0.1638017	0.1665552	0.4365233	0.4621948
	(0.2255876)	(0.2212689)	(0.3604608)	(0.3563759)
Prop_black	0.3179146*	0.3244374	0.1845149	0.9903776[c]
	(0.159529)	(0.1708367)	(0.2762411)	(0.559942)
Avg_hrs_wk	-0.005215	-0.0049215	-0.0071548	-0.0084913
	(0.0081877)	(0.0088342)	(0.0115993)	(0.0123685)
Avg_yrs_exp	-0.0070326	-0.0072369	-0.0246123*	-0.0239397
	(0.0113757)	(0.0089951)	(0.0119829)	(0.0138859)
Agri[a]			0.2150454	0.1217026
			(0.1615696)	(0.1650909)
Trade			-0.0370916	-0.0295094
			(0.1070549)	(0.0965883)
Service			-0.0840773	-0.094419
			(0.1309401)	(0.129793)
Finance			-0.0851385	0.2581358
			(0.1259547)	(0.2085117)
No. of observations	50	50	50	50
R^2	0.2782	0.2783	0.3245	0.3805

* indicates significance at a 0.05 level.
[a]Manufacturing is the omitted industrial category.
[b]Significant at $p = 0.071$ level.
[c]Significant at $p = 0.062$ level.

per annum, is found (significant at a $p = .081$ level). The one statistically significant effect on the white gender wage gap when the full set of covariates is included is "average years of experience." Women appear to suffer a greater wage disadvantage in settings in which average experience is greater. The same tendency, though of smaller magnitude and significant only at a $p = .086$ level, is found for blacks. For colored workers, the effect of being in a more experienced work force appears to work in the opposite direction, reducing the gender wage gap. A possible explanation will be presented in the discussion section of this chapter.

For whites, there is no observed effect of unionization on the wage gap, but for colored, when the full set of covariates is included, it appears to increase the gender wage differential (though the coefficient is only significant at a $p = 0.071$ level). For blacks, the union effect of widening the gender wage gap is significant in specifications (1) and (2) but drops out when sector fixed effects and the time trend variable are added. Black women also appear to suffer less of a wage penalty in agriculture and trade, compared with manufacturing, the base industrial category.

It should be noted that there are almost certainly unobserved factors which vary by gender that have not been accounted for in this analysis. These are likely to include selection issues with respect to both exclusion from the labor market and exclusion from the employed labor force. It is therefore likely that the observed gender wage gaps are an underestimate of the level that would be found if all factors could be taken into account. For instance, it is likely that women with more than average unmeasured human capital endowments (ability, energy, and/or quality of education) will disproportionately select themselves into the formal labor market, and it is also likely that they will be more able to overcome employer discrimination with respect to hiring.

3.4 Estimation Procedure: Female/Male Employment Ratios

Given the high unemployment rates in South Africa in the decade 1995–2004, it seemed useful to extend this study to an investigation of trends in the employment of women over this period. For each year, the ratio of female to male employees was computed (See Table 3). Proportions are computed separately for each racial group in each of the five industrial sectors for each of the 10 years, using the household and worker surveys that are employed in the Stage I wage gap regressions. The analysis of the female/male employment ratios uses a similar strategy to that used in the two-stage gender-wage-gap regressions. In the regression analysis, the proportions of female/male workers in each year and industrial sector are used as the dependent variables in the employment ratio regressions[6] As in the case of wage-differential analysis, separate regressions are run for each of the three main racial groups (See Tables 4a–4c). Specification (1) controls only for time (year). Specification (2) includes only FDI/k as a control. Specification (3) employs worker characteristics (proportion of workers unionized, proportion female, proportion black, average hours per week worked, and average years of experience) as controls. Specification (4) adds the globalization variable (FDI/k) and sector fixed effects to the set of control variables included in (3); and specification (5) adds the variable "year" to the set of control variables included in (4).

Table 3. Stage I: female/male employees by year, race, and sector

	Year and race	*Agriculture*	*Manufacturing*	*Trade*	*Services*	*Finance*
1995	White	0.226	0.228	0.480	0.543	0.588
		(168)	(707)	(986)	(1541)	(740)
	Black	0.182	0.319	0.465	0.499	0.351
		(3,286)	(1,914)	(1,931)	(3,931)	(439)
	Colored	0.279	0.448	0.556	0.503	0.471
		(1,076)	(878)	(858)	(967)	(202)
1996	White	0.569	0.543	0.575	0.587	0.575
		(1,951)	(2,180)	(2,155)	(2,382)	(2,198)
	Black	0.598	0.595	0.602	0.602	0.603
		(25,960)	(26,317)	(26,235)	(27,195)	(25,619)
	Colored	0.594	0.604	0.625	0.615	0.626
		(2,413)	(2,477)	(2,406)	(2,529)	2,228)
1997	White	0.429	0.267	0.357	0.462	0.398
		(2,646)	(960)	(947)	(1,317)	(945)
	Black	0.2403	0.383	0.476	0.612	0.436
		(3,288)	(3,806)	(3,545)	(6,852)	(2,289)
	Colored	0.351	0.410	0.501	0.558	0.389
		(1,184)	(895)	(789)	(1,355)	(373)
1998	White	0.605	0.590	0.589	0.627	0.592
		(2030)	(2,251)	(2,401)	(2,539)	(2,450)
	Black	0.592	0.596	0.602	0.615	0.603
		(27,897)	(27,800)	(28,470)	(29,888)	(3,903)
	Colored	0.590	0.605	0.615	0.623	0.62.0
		(3,653)	(3,645)	(3,653)	(3,903)	(3,344)
1999	White	0.583	0.571	0.586	0.623	0.595
		(2,487)	(2,673)	(2,893)	(3,026)	(2,917)
	Black	0.587	0.588	0.593	0.596	0.595
		(37,829)	(37,712)	(38,777)	(38,720)	(36,498)
	Colored	0.581	0.617	0.624	0.619	0.631
		(5,157)	(4,796)	(4,809)	(4,808)	(4,405)
2000	White	0.595	0.589	0.589	0.635	0.601
		(1,976)	(2,103)	(2,321)	(2,444)	(2,256)
	Black	0.583	0.583	0.591	0.592	0.590
		(36,706)	(36,137)	(37,606)	(36,930)	(34,804)
	Colored	0.583	0.624	0.626	0.635	0.639
		(4,994)	(4,669)	(4,655)	(4,579)	(4,264)
2001	White	0.588	0.575	0.581	0.630	0.596
		(2,274)	(2,541)	(2,700)	(2,847)	(2,678)
	Black	0.580	0.584	0.590	0.583	0.590
		(37,942)	(38,063)	(39,620)	(39,032)	36,843)
	Colored	0.583	0.614	0.623	0.626	0.630
		(5,175)	(4,986)	(4,946)	(4,923)	(4,592)

(*continued*)

Table 3. (continued)

	Year and race	*Agriculture*	*Manufacturing*	*Trade*	*Services*	*Finance*
2002	White	0.570	0.549	0.586	0.597	0.544
		(1,854)	(2,086)	(2,131)	(2,294)	(2,176)
	Black	0.564	0.564	0.569	0.571	0.586
		(28.642)	(28.861)	29,765)	(29,830)	(28,001)
	Colored	0.552	0.579	0.583	0.584	0.589
		(4,279)	(4,139)	(4,021)	(4,114)	(3,762)
2003	White	0.607	0.586	0.597	0.649	0.608
		(2,464)	(2,740)	(2,914)	(3.069)	(2,877)
	Black	0.573	0.580	0.585	0.586	0.583
		(35,383)	(35,221)	(36,571)	(36,526)	(34,349)
	Colored	0.566	0.595	0.607	0.608	0.611
		(4,997)	(4,770)	(4,750)	(4,765)	(4,395)
2004	White	0.593	0.581	0.596	0.638	0.624
		(2,323)	(2,507)	(2,754)	(2,818)	(2,574)
	Black	0.581	0.586	0.590	0.593	0.589
		(39,619)	(39,364)	(40,628)	(40,418)	(38,237)
	Colored	0.575	0.601	0.616	0.608	0.616
		(6,526)	(6,157)	(6,328)	(6,387)	(5,837)

Note: Sample sizes are shown in parentheses under the proportions.

3.5 *Empirical Results: Employment Ratios*

The results of this analysis are shown in Tables 4a–4c. When only the time trend was considered, all three racial groups showed highly significant gains over the decade in the ratio of women to men employees. However, only white women were found to have statistically significant gains in employment share over the decade when the full set of control variables was included. For colored and blacks, when the full set of covariates is included, there is no evidence of a time trend in women's share of the employment. Black women tend to comprise a smaller proportion of the work force in circumstances where the average years of experience is higher. (This is only marginally significant at a $p = 0.09$ level.) This is true for colored women workers in specification (3) of the model, but the effect disappears when industry fixed effects and FDI/k are added. For all three racial groups, there is some evidence that women comprise a higher proportion of in an environment where the proportion of black coworkers is higher. Although these results are significant in specification (4) of the model, in all three cases the effect disappears when "year" is added.

Table 4a. Employment proportion female: white

Independent variables	*(1)*	*(2)*	*(3)*	*(4)*	*(5)*
Year	0.017936**				0.019910*
	(0.00503)				(0.007549)
Prop_FDI		0.015178*		0.036837	0.008595
		(0.006272)		(0.019853)	(0.019366)
Prop_union			0.01721	0.10940	−0.039779
			(0.138318)	(0.23397)	(0.215874)
Prop_female			0.399143[b]	0.673664	−0.652251
			(0.209481)	(0.465878)	(0.41959)
Prop_black			0.023391	0.578039*	−0.094132
			(0.088433)	(0.274495)	(0.34661)
Avg_hrs_wk			0.00917	−0.009048	−0.007935
			(0.002003)	(0.010502)	(0.010258)
Avg_yrs_exp			−0.00442	−0.010333	−0.010894
			(006111)	(0.012550)	(0.011215)
Agri[a]				0.035919	0.113779
				(0.101489)	(0.106261)
Trade				-0.083748	−0.09007[b]
				(0.094193)	(0.082752)
Service				−0.104018	−0.095398
				(0.13870)	(0.130554)
Finance				−0.222505*	−0.06382
				(0.094565)	(0.120126)
No. of observations	50	50	50	50	50
R^2	0.2802	0.0461	0.1622	0.4007	0.4770

* indicates significance at a 0.05 level.
** indicates significance at a 0.01 level.
[a]Manufacturing is the omitted industrial category.
[b]Significant at as $p = 0.06$ level.

Table 4b. Employment proportion female: black

Independent variables	*(1)*	*(2)*	*(3)*	*(4)*	*(5)*
Year	0.015416*				0.007625
	(0.005091)				(0.005982)
Prop_FDI		0.013045*		0.020167	0.021108
		(0.005649)		(0.01842)	(0.026486)
Prop_union			0.047247	−0.068332	−0.015761
			(0.124987)	(0.137894)	(0.520526)
Prop_female			0.222465	0.659057	0.50115
			(0.18664)	0.517421)	(0.520526)
Prop_black			0.137361	0.64677*	0.389367
			(0.104066)	(0.234979)	(0.288403)
Avg_hrs_wk			0.005684	−0.009065	−0.008638
			(0.8592987)	(0.014902)	0.014965)
Avg_yrs_exp			−0.01420[b]	−0.0159[c]	−0.016114[d]
			(0.00727)	(0.009151)	(0.008882)
Agri[a]				−0.03042	−0.000605
				(0.116134)	(0.120873)
Trade				−0.09539	−0.097808
				(0.077017)	(0.076859)
Service				−0.099948	−0.096657
				(0.160684)	(0.1600877)
Finance				0.183441*	0.073795
				(0.081549)	(0.115373)
No. of observations	50	50	50	50	50
R^2	0.2191	0.0362	02080	0.3994	0.4112

* indicates significance at a 0.05 level.
[a]Manufacturing is the omitted industrial category.
[b]Significant at p = 0.057 level.
[c]Significant at p = 0.09 level.
[d]Significant at p = 0.078 level.

Table 4c. Employment proportion female: colored

Independent variables	*(1)*	*(2)*	*(3)*	*(4)*	*(5)*
Year	0.011824*				0.007526
	(0.003897)				(0.005236)
Prop_FDI		0.00765		0.030709	0.020033
		(0.005063)		(0.158919)	(0.018703)
Prop_union			0.074398	0.158919	0.102527
			(0.098255)	(0.117593)	(0.123669)
Prop_female			0.178673	0.502442	0.494348
			(0.145763)	(0.364757)	(0.355463)
Prop_black			0.061854	0.461585*	0.207493
			(0.088984)	(0.187999)	(0.240398)
Avg_hrs_wk			0.005282	−0.010005	−0.009584
			(0.007174)	(0.010714)	(0.010733)
Avg_yrs_exp			−0.104991*	−0,004489	−0.004701
			(0.005234)	(0.008337)	(0.008073)
Agri[a]				−0.01724	0.012191
				(0.086185)	(0.090088)
Trade				−0.043367	−0.045758
				(0.059074)	(0.057534)
Service				−0.13654	−0.133282
				(0.111508)	(0.11047)
Finance				0.165016*	0.056781
				(0.061664)	(0.089412)
No. of observations	50	50	50	50	50
R^2	0.1982	0.0191	0.2117	0.3835	0.4013

* indicates significance at a 0.05 level.
[a]Manufacturing is the omitted industrial category.

The issue of a possible trade-off between employment opportunities and wages is investigated by looking at the correlations between the magnitude of the wage gap and the ratio of female to male workers. The results are shown in Table 5. A positive correlation between the size of the gender wage gap and the proportion of women workers is observed for both the black and colored samples. However, for white workers this does not seem to apply. For whites there is even a negative correlation between the ratio of female to male workers and the wage differential. One factor that may be relevant is the small proportion of the South African labor force consisting of whites.[7]

Table 5. Correlations between ln wage differentials and proportion of women employed

Variable	*ln M/F wage diff*	*% Women emp*	*Year*
a. White			
ln M/F wage diff	1.000		
% Women emp	−0.0626	1.000	
Year	−0.5294	−0.1591	1.000
b. Black			
ln M/F wage diff	1.000		
% Women emp	0.1082	1.000	
Year	0.4680	0.0856	1.000
C. Colored			
ln M/F wage diff	1.000		
% Women emp	0.1987	1.000	
Year	0.4452	−0.1160	1.000

4 Discussion

For colored workers, the gender gap in wages was observed to narrow significantly over the decade by about 2.4 percent per annum. Although no statistically significant temporal effect was found for white workers in the period 1995–2004, about a 7.5 percent annual decline in the wage gap was observed, significant at a $p = 0.10$ level. For black workers the gender wage differential was approximately equal in magnitude to that of colored workers but only significant at a $p = 0.08$ level. A decline in the gender wage gap for black and colored workers may have been in part related to the extension of the minimum wage in 2002 to cover the domestic sector, since women of color constitute the majority of domestic workers in South Africa.[8] Although the service sector data used in this analysis exclude personal services, there could have been some spillover effects on wages of other low-skill female workers. A noticeable positive effect of the enactment of this legislation would, however, be surprising, given the weak machinery for enforcement of the law (Dinkelman and Ranchhod 2012, 29).

Another factor affecting the gender wage gap for black and coloured workers may be related to a racial difference in returns to education, favoring non-whites. The largest increase in the female labor force was in a demographic described as "African female first-time job seekers who were urban, under 35 years of age, and possessing some level of secondary education" (Bhorat and Oosthuizen 2005, 6). It is known that at least at the beginning of the period studied the returns to education were much higher for non-whites than for whites. Mwabu and Schultz found the returns to high school education in 1993 for all non-whites to be approximately twice the returns for white men. They also report higher wages in urban than in rural areas, and the colored population was heavily concentrated in urban areas, particularly old Cape province (Mwabu and Schultz 2000, 316). The large influx into the labor market of high school educated non-white urban women might then result in a compression of the non-white gender wage gap (Schultz et al. 1988).

Being employed in a sector with a higher proportion of black workers appears to be associated with a higher female to male employment ratio. The effect is significant for all three racial groups in specification (4) of the model, but when time is introduced in specification (5) the effect appears to vanish. It is nonetheless an interesting phenomenon that bears further investigation and may be suggestive that sectors of the economy that are less racially discriminating may also be more accepting of women.

The degree of globalization (measured in this study by the FDI/capital stock ratio) has often been thought to be associated with wider wage differentials. If women are on average in less skilled jobs and have less labor market experience, they would likely be affected by this. However, this factor was not found to be significant in any specifications of the model nor for any racial group. This is not surprising since this study looks at the "pure" or residual gender wage gap, adjusting for individual workers' education, occupation, and experience. Thus the portion of the wage differential associated with skill difference, often thought to be larger in the tradable sectors, has been at least partially adjusted for in the residual gender wage differentials estimated in this chapter.

For whites, the proportion of women in the employed labor force shows strong and robust growth over the decade under investigation. In the case of black and colored workers, this phenomenon disappears when sector characteristics and fixed effects are introduced, although it is significant when time is the only covariate included in the model tested. These findings, at least for white women, are similar to what has been reported about the post-NAFTA period in Mexico. Mexico, like South Africa, faced very high rates of unemployment after its transition to a more open economy. In Mexico the male/female wage differential was stable between 1990 and 2000, but the proportion of women in the employed labor force increased, so women's share of the total wage bill increased (Aguayo-Tellez et al. 2010). Trade liberalization in Mexico appears to have favored the employment of women over men. Aguayo-Tellez et al. explain this phenomenon as the result of outsourcing to Mexico, and an increase in assembly-type activity. This explanation does not seem to apply to South Africa, but a fairly simple alternative explanation seems plausible: with extremely high unemployment rates and persistent, if declining, gender gaps in wages, why shouldn't firms hire women workers if they are cheaper than their male counterparts?

The fact that the improvement over the decade in the female proportion of workers was only statistically significant for white women is consistent with the widely held notion that South African black and colored women workers are largely limited to employment in low-level jobs, many of which require physically demanding work for which women may not be deemed suitable (Casale 2004). Moreover, white women undoubtedly comprised a very small proportion of the labor force, at least at the beginning of the period being studied. That low initial base could be at least part of the reason for their improvement as a proportion of employed workers over the decade.

In conclusion, it appears that white women workers' gains over the first post-apartheid decade are primarily in employment, whereas the main gains for non-white, particularly for colored, women are primarily in the form of a decline in the wage gap relative to their male counterparts. It may be the case that affirmative action with respect to race has had some positive spillover effects on the decline in the gender wage gap for non-whites. But it is also likely that the large influx of relatively better educated colored women entering the labor force were able to command higher wages.

It is unlikely that gender-based wage differentials will entirely disappear as long as unemployment in South Africa remains high and female unemployment rates far exceed those of males. It appears that the opening up of the South African economy that accompanied the end of apartheid on balance negatively affected opportunities for workers. It augmented the substitution of capital for labor and the expansion of capital intensive industries and led to the modification of some of the anti-discriminatory pro-labor policies that were introduced in the mid-1990s. Many women undoubtedly entered the labor force to supplement family income in the face of declining employment opportunities for males. This in turn contributed to the persistence of high unemployment rates, particularly for non-whites.

It is nonetheless encouraging to find some evidence of improvement in the gender wage gap and in the proportion of women in the employed labor force at a time in history when attention was focused on racial discrimination.

However, an important question that has not been addressed in this chapter is the effect on the welfare of households that has accompanied these apparent improvements in labor market opportunities for women. Family incomes may still be declining if women earners are simply substituting in the labor market for their higher paid, but unemployed, spouses.

Notes

1. Barbara Bergmann, however, has pointed out that the issue of including sex was seriously debated and that it was included under the leadership of Rep. Martha Griffiths. But clearly this it a controversial issue (Bergmann 2010, 104).
2. Equations were also estimated for Asians. However, as the Asian sample size was very small in some sectors and years, results are reported only for white, black, and colored workers. Results for Asians are available on request.
3. Ahmed et al. attribute this unusual balance in capital flows to South Africa's foreign currency reserves, and also, particularly in 1997–2000, to South Africa's absorbing of the portfolio outflows from East Asia and Latin America (Ahmed et al. 2007, 277).
4. The OHS (Statistics South Africa, 1995–1999) was funded by the governments of Denmark, the Netherlands, and Norway under the auspices of the World Bank. It was discontinued after 1999.
5. As this chapter is comparing women and men of the same race, when constructing the gender-effect variable, the issue of difference in quality of education is deemed to be relatively unimportant. By contrast, if this were a chapter on racial wage differentials, the importance of unobserved quality differences in education would make using "number of years of education completed" a much more inadequate measure of education.
6. The sample sizes used to compute each of these Stage I ratios are shown in parentheses in Table 3.
7. A snapshot of the South African Labour Force in 1995 and 2002 shows whites comprising 14.4 percent of the labor force in 1995 and 11.8 percent in 2002 (Bhorat and Oosthuizen 2005, Table 3, p. 5).
8. Domestic workers constitute 18 percent of female employment and women constitute 80 percent of domestic workers (Dinkelman and Ranchhod 2012, 29).

References

Aguayo-Tellez, E., et al. 2010. "Did Trade Liberalization Help Women? The Case of Mexico in the 1990's," NBER Working Paper w16195.

Ahmed, F., R. Arezki, and N. Funke. 2007. "The Composition of Capital Flows to South Africa," *Journal of International Development* 19(2): 276–294.

Bejuidenhout, A. et al. 2007. ""Globalization and Poverty: Impacts on Households of Employment and Restructuring in the Textiles Industry of South Africa," *Journal of International Development* 19: 545–565.

Bergmann, B. 2010. *The Economic Emergence of Women*. 2nd edn. New York: Palgrave Macmillan.

Bhorat, H., and M. Oosthuizen. 2005. "The Post-Apartheid South African Labour Market," Development Policy Research Unit Working Paper 05/93, School of Economics, University of Cape Town.

Bhorat, H. et al. 2012. "Institutional Wage Effects: Revisiting Union and Bargaining Council Wage Premia in South Africa," *South African Journal of Economics* 80(3): 400–414.

Casale, D. 2004. "What Has the Feminization of the Labour Market 'Bought' Women in South Africa? Trends in Labour Force Participation, Employment and Earnings, 1995–2001," *Journal of Interdisciplinary Economics* 15(3–4): 251–275.

Casale, D., and D. Posel 2011. "Unions and the Gender Wage Gap in South Africa," *Journal of African Economics* 10(1): 27–59.

Dinkelman, T., and V. Ranchhod. 2012. "Evidence on the Impact of Minimum Wage Laws in an Informal Sector: Domestic Workers in South Africa," *Journal of Development Economics* 99: 27–45.

Edwards, C. 2004. "Restructuring the New South Africa: Review Article," *International Review of Applied Economics* 9(1): 101–108.

Figini, P., and Holger Gorg. 2011. "Does Foreign Direct Investment Affect Wage Inequality? An Empirical Investigation," *The World Economy* 34(9): 1455–1474.

Funke, N., Faisal Ahmed, and Rabah Arezki. 2005. "The Composition of Capital Flows: Is South Africa Different?" IMF Working Papers, 05/40.

Grun, C. 2004. "Direct and Indirect Gender Discrimination in the South African Labour Market," *International Journal of Manpower* 25(3–4): 321–342.

Hinks, T. 2002. "Gender Wage Differentials and Discrimination in the New South Africa," *Applied Economics* 34(16): 2043–2052.

International Labor Organization. 2000–2004. *Labour Force Surveys for South Africa*. ILO. www.ilo.org/dyn/lfsurvey/lfsurvey.home.

Jenkins, R. 2004. "Globalization, Production, Employment, and Poverty: Debates and Evidence," *Journal of International Development* 16(1): 1–12.

Jenkins, R. 2006. "Globalization and the Labour Market in South Africa," *Journal of International Development* 18(July): 649–664.

Mwabu, Germano, and Schultz, T. Paul. 2000. "Wage Premiums for Education and Location of South African Workers, by Gender and Race," *Economic Development and Cultural Change* 48(2): 452–460.

Ntuli, M. 2012. "Investigating the Gender Gap in South African Trade Union Membership: A Decomposition Analysis," *South African Journal of Economics* 80(1): 42–61.

Ntuli, M., and P. Kwenda. 2014. " Labour Unions and Wage Inequality Among African Men in South Africa," *Development South Africa* 31(2): 322–346.

Schultz, T. Paul et al. 1998. Wage Premia for Education and Location, By Gender and Race in South Africa. Yale Economic Growth Center, Center Discussion Papers, New Haven, Connecticut.

Serumaga-Zake, P., and Willem Naude. 2001. "Labour Market Discrimination in the North West Province of South Africa," *Development South Africa* 18(5): 671–682.

Statistics South Africa. 1995–1999. *October Household Surveys (OHS)*. Pretoria, South Africa: Statistics South Africa (producer); Pretoria: South African Data Archive (distributor).

Van Der Berg, S., et al. 2007. "Post-Apartheid South Africa: Poverty and Distribution Trends in an Era of Globalization," NU-WIDER Research Paper RP2007/57.

Wakeford, J. 2004. "The Productivity-Wage Relationship in South Africa: An Empirical Investigation," *Development Southern Africa* 21(1): 109–113.

Shirley Johnson-Lans is Professor of Economics at Vassar College. Her principal areas of teaching and research are Labor Economics, Health Care Economics, Gender Issues in Economics, and Income Inequality. Her publications include many journal articles and book chapters spanning a wide variety of subjects, from child marriage in rural India to an analysis of the Affordable Care Act. She is the author of the widely used textbook, *A Health Economics Primer* (Pearson: Addison-Wesley, 2006) which she is currently revising. She received her Ph.D. in Economics from Columbia University.

Index

S. Johnson-Lans (ed.), *Wage Inequality in Africa*, Global Perspectives on Wealth and Distribution, DOI 10.1007/978-3-319-51565-6